The Mobile Phone Revolution in Morocco

The Mobile Phone Revolution in Morocco

Cultural and Economic Transformations

Hsain Ilahiane

LEXINGTON BOOKS
Lanham • Boulder • New York • London

Chapter 1 is a revised version of an earlier published journal article. Hsain Ilahiane and John Sherry, "Joutia: Street Vendor Entrepreneurship and the Informal Economy of Information and Communication Technologies in Morocco," *The Journal of North African Studies* Volume 13, Issue 2 (2008); pp. 243–255, https://doi.org/10.1080/13629380801996570.

Chapter 2 is a revised version of an earlier published journal article. Hsain Ilahiane and John, Sherry. "The Problematics of the 'Bottom of the Pyramid' Approach to International Development: The Case of Micro-entrepreneurs' Use of Mobile Phones in Morocco." *International Technologies and International Development* 8, no. 1 (2012): 13–26.

Chapter 3 is a revised version of an earlier published book chapter. Hsain Ilahiane. "The Berber House or the World Leaked: Mobile Phones, Gender Switching, and Place in Morocco," in *Location Technologies in International Context*, edited by Rowan Wilk, Gerard Goggin, and Heather Horst (New York: Routledge, 2019), 54–66.

Published by Lexington Books
An imprint of The Rowman & Littlefield Publishing Group, Inc.
4501 Forbes Boulevard, Suite 200, Lanham, Maryland 20706
www.rowman.com

86-90 Paul Street, London EC2A 4NE

Copyright © 2022 by The Rowman & Littlefield Publishing Group, Inc.

British Library Cataloguing in Publication Information Available

Library of Congress Cataloging-in-Publication Data on File

ISBN 978-1-7936-1660-9 (pbk)
ISBN 978-1-7936-1658-6 (cloth)
ISBN 978-1-7936-1659-3 (electronic)

Contents

List of Figures

Acknowledgments

Anthropological fieldwork and research involve considerable teamwork, and there are many organizations and people who have contributed, directly or indirectly, to this project. I would like to express my gratitude to Intel Corporation for funding this project and to my colleagues and friends, John W. Sherry and Tony Salvador, and the social sciences team at Intel Corporation in Beaverton, Oregon.

To the government of Morocco I owe gratitude for permission to work in Mohammedia, Rabat, and Errachidia, and for much help and cooperation I found in L'Institut National des Postes et Télécommunications (INPT), Telecom Partners, Maroc Télécom, Meditel Télécom, Secretariat d'Etat auprés du Premier Ministère Chargé de la Poste et des Technologies des Télécommunications et de l'Information (SEPTI), the Agence Nationale de Réglementation des Télécommunications (ARNT), L'Institut Agronomique et Vétérinaire Hassan II, and the Office Regional de Mise en Valeur Agricole du Tafilalet in Errachidia. Among the many people who have provided illuminating discussions on mobile phone use in Morocco and the United States, I would especially like to thank Ahmed Abbadi, Noureddine Ait Menna, Fadma Ait Mous, Ken Anderson, El Houssain Baali, Richard Beckwith, Lorna Butler, Abdellatif Bencherifa, the late Michael Bonine, Yahia Bouabdellaoui, Mohamed Abdelfattah Charif Chefchaouni, Nabil Chbouki, Daoud Fanissi, Abdellah Hammoudi, Ahmed Herzenni, Said Ilahiane, Marcia Inhorn, Kathi Kitner, Scott Mainwaring, Wendy March, Mustapha Qadery, Thomas Park, Hassan Rachik, Abderrahmane Rachik, and Ahmed Toufiq.

But my greatest debt is to the farmers of the Errachidia region, street ven- dors of the old city *suq* in Rabat, and the skilled workers, or *hrayfiyyah*, of the shantytowns of Mohammedia, who made me welcome and allowed me to pry into their mobile phones, relations, homes, fields, and work sites. Finally, I thank my wife, Ann Becker, for her support and patience. To all these indi- viduals and organizations, I am grateful.

Note on Transliteration

It is generally recognized that efforts at transliterating North African vernacular terms and proper names and places, whether Berber or Arabic, present a real challenge for nonnative speakers of North African languages. To make sense of these terms, I have followed the conventions of the *International Journal of Middle East Studies*. For Arabic and Berber, the consonant *kh* is pronounced as in *Bach*, and *gh* as the French *r*. The Arabic *'ain* has been rendered with ', and the *hamza*, the glottal stop diacritical mark, with `. Place names and common proper names with English and French spellings appear as they do in English and French and are not transliterated. Thus, Errachidia, not Rrachidia or al-rachidia; Qur'an, not Quran.

Introduction

The Mobile Phone Is the
Total Social Artifact

INTRODUCTION

The mobile phone. It goes by many names in Morocco: "telephone *noofus*" (handheld phone) or "*agru njeeb*" (frog of the pocket) in Tamazight (Berber); "*al-portable*" in Moroccan Arabic or "*le portable*" (the portable) in French. Unlike other technologies before it, it is a low-cost, portable, real-time, always-on, point-to-point communication device that has become the manifestation of the "digital age" for much of the world. In two decades of its commercial viability, the mobile phone has become an essential part of the everyday life of billions of people, and it has been one of the most transformative technologies in the world, particularly in the global South.

According to the 2019 International Telecommunication Union Report, there were 8.3 billion mobile phone subscriptions worldwide by the end of 2018—with a global population of 7.7 billion—with 2.71 billion of these subscriptions being smartphones. Between 1998 and 2020, most Moroccans went from no phone ownership to ownership of a mobile phone. In the past two decades, mobile phone subscriptions in Morocco rose from 0.12 million subscriptions in 1998 to 44.74 million subscriptions in 2018, with a penetration rate of about 131 percent, whereas the number of landline users in Morocco stood at 2.04 million in 2018, with a penetration rate of about 6.12 percent (ARNT 2018; ITU 2019). This remarkable adoption rate can best be understood as the result of several major contributing factors, all of which will be examined in this book: the major economic reforms undertaken by the Moroccan state in the mid-1980s and 1990s, technological innovation, and the business models associated with the ease of use and utility of the mobile phone.

This extraordinary penetration rate of mobile telephony in Morocco, as elsewhere in the developing world, underscores the degree to which this new technology has become part of everyday routines and serves various communicative and economic needs. In this book, I shed light on mobile phone use *in practice* through ethnographic and survey research conducted with Moroccan men and women in a wide range of settings in 2003, 2012, and 2016. I am concerned with ways in which Moroccans use the mobile phone as a tool to organize a newly networked work and social life. My analysis is limited to feature or basic mobile phones, not smartphones. Feature or basic mobile phones are sometimes called "dumb phones." They provide voice calling and text messaging functionality as well as limited internet and multimedia capabilities. The feature phones I focus on in this study lacked internet connectivity but included basic software such as games, camera, calendar, and calculator applications. My goal is to analyze economic and social life by focusing on the ways in which Moroccans use the mobile phone to negotiate emergent economic and social relationships. I examine the ways it is used to define new forms of entrepreneurship in the informal sector, farming, and domestic labor. Furthermore, I address how Moroccans use the mobile phone to reframe core notions of gender and space, honor and shame, placemaking, and surveillance and control.

Specifically, I underscore the relevance of the themes of entrepreneurship, economic productivity, development, labor, gender, surveillance, place, and social change in this ethnography. I highlight how Moroccan men and women engage in emergent forms of mobile phone sociability in their quest to create meaningful social and economic lives. In so doing, I render the everyday lives of these men and women visible and provide empirical evidence for the positive economic difference the mobile phone is making in their lives—thereby demonstrating, in a concrete way, not only the social impacts of mobile phone use but also its compelling economic effects. Filled with rich ethnographic stories of how urban and rural Moroccans put mobile phones to social and economic use, I enable readers to contemplate the economic productivity of mobile phone users, as well as the social and cultural challenges facing them in a Muslim context in the twenty-first century. I address the practices and everyday-life engagements of Muslim men and women with mobile phones in a variety of economic and cultural settings, while, at the same time, showing how they are responding to technological and social transformations. The Moroccan men and women I present in this book include urban street vendors, urban micro-entrepreneurs, urban female domestic workers, and smallholder farmers, all of whom are responding to the social and economic transformation brought on by the introduction of and their engagement with the mobile phone.

In the literature on mobile telephony, mobile phone studies have been framed by what Donners (2010) calls a "dual heritage": mobile phones are either studied through the lens of their social impacts or their economic benefits, usually privileging one of these approaches over the other. In general, mobile phone studies positioned within the framework of Information and Communication Technology for Development (ICT4D) tend to focus on the use of the mobile phone to produce specific economic goals such as increasing productivity of goods and services and users' incomes; what Donner calls "embedded directionality." Donner (2009) also highlights the blurring of livelihoods and lives in mobile phone usage, including their value and use for social and economic activities. Anthropologists and other social scientists, however, emphasize the cultural and social consequences of mobile telephony: for example, in youth fashion, style, and body image (Fortunati 2005); in sociality, local and nonlocal "link-up" networks, sex, and economic survival (Horst and Miller 2006); in business networks and entrepreneurship (Donner 2006; Ilahiane and Sherry 2012); in "micro-coordination," "softening of schedules," and flexibility (Ling 2004); in "meaningful mobilities" and reworking of gender, class, caste, power, agency, labor, and location dynamics in trans-hierarchical settings (Tenhunen 2008; Tacchi et al. 2012; Tacchi 2014; Doron and Jeffrey 2013; Servaes 2014; Costa 2016, 2019); in privacy, secrecy, intimacy, romance, and trust (Archambault 2017); in the political economy of telecommunications and the moral economy of gifting and sharing of mobile phone services (Foster and Horst 2018); and in leisure, romance, gaming, and digital literacies (Arora 2010, 2019).

Mobile phones, be they smartphones or basic feature phones, are seen as essential tools for and of social change because they allow connectivity for billions of people. That said, my ethnographic and survey research on everyday use of mobile phones in Morocco points to a range of implications that go beyond the "dual heritage" and "monolithic visions" framings of mobile technology impacts on society and economy (Donner 2010; Ling and Horst 2011; Tacchi 2014; Costa 2016; Rangaswamy and Arora 2016; Horst 2021). In this book, I move away from the binary focus of mobile phones as either objects of economic development or social and cultural transformation; instead, I view mobile phones as *total social artifacts* that are deeply imbricated into peoples' livelihoods and lives, as is made evident through their everyday use in various mixtures of economic, social, and cultural activities in Morocco. It is important to reframe the binary or linear understanding of social/cultural transformation and economic development, especially normative understanding of mobile phones and their users in the global South. I argue that mobile phones as *total social artifacts* are not just simple objects for social change. My argument runs against the rigid dichotomy between culture/society and economy used in the study of mobile phones.

Like other modernization technologies such as the Green Revolution and mechanization of agriculture in the 1950s (Lewis and Gardner 2015; Crewe and Axelby 2013), the snowmobile in the 1960s (Pelto 1973), the truck in the 1970s (Chatty 1996), and the internet in the 1990s (Castells 1996; Miller and Slater 2000), mobile phones have emerged as one of the defining technologies in the ongoing great economic and social transformations of our time (Horst 2021; Miller et al. 2021). In this introduction, first, I use Latour's actor network theory (ANT), along with Marcel Mauss' central notion of total social fact, to reposition the theoretical framing and understanding of the place and role of mobile phones in people's lives and livelihoods. I argue that the mobile phone is not only a total social fact but also a *total social artifact*. Second, I provide a narrative of the global and local contexts of telecommunications and key technological and marketing innovations behind the rapid uptake of mobile phones in Morocco since the late 1980s and 1990s. Third, I provide a description of the areas where I conducted my ethnographic research for this study. Finally, I describe the methods of the study and the organization of the book.

THE MOBILE PHONE AS A TOTAL SOCIAL ARTIFACT

In order to have a comprehensive understanding of the impacts of the mobile phone on people's livelihoods and lives, I am proposing the concept of a *total social artifact* as a lens through which to view the impacts of mobile telephony. This concept brings together elements of Bruno Latour's ANT and Mauss' notion of total social fact. Through the lens of the total social artifact the mobile phone can be viewed as having impacts on almost every aspect of people's lives and livelihoods.

Unlike technological determinism studies (Sclove 1995; Winner 1980) in which technological artifacts are seen as powerful determinants of human behavior, and social constructivism analyses (Pfaffenberger 1992; Pinch and Bijker 1987) in which technological artifacts are viewed as passive and powerless in shaping social action, even though technical artifacts appear to play the role of intermediaries in all sorts of social activities, Latour and his colleagues argue that societies are not only maintained by social relations and institutions but by technological artifacts as well (Callon, Law and Rip 1986; Callon 1987; Latour 1992; Callon and Latour 1992; Akrich 1992; Ilahiane and Venter 2016). Latour argues that technological artifacts prescribe behaviors, induce cultural beliefs and practices, and shape aspects of their social context. In Latour's view, no difference should be made between humans and artifacts; all are actors, or *actants*, that are able to act, mediate, delegate, compose, extend, and influence. Actants are given competencies, that is, powers and capacities to act. The competencies of actants in a setting cannot be determined in advance but can only be attributed to them as the result of their being embedded in a network of human and nonhuman entities. The entire distinction between human actors and physical objects, physical capacities and behavioral dispositions, physical processes and human actions, and physical laws and social norms or habits disappears; there is only an interplay of actants and their performances, which are all described in the same terms (Latour 2005).

Similarly, Mauss, in his classic work *The Gift*, develops the notion of a total social fact. He argues that gift exchange in traditional societies, which involved practices such as potlatches among North American Indians or the Kula ring among Melanesian islanders, was not only complex and polyvalent but also constituted the basis of economic life, creating social bonds between groups, and was part of a "total system" (in French *préstation totale*). The gift, as Mauss views it, is more than a simple commodity exchange, and it is a "total social fact" which metonymically represents every domain of the society it is part of. The gift is economic, kinship-oriented, political, legal, mythological, religious, magical, practical, personal, and social. By moving such an object through the social landscape, the gift-giver through the act of giving rearranges the fabric of sociality and creates the obligation of reciprocity, and it is this that constitutes the core of the gift's power.

Like the notion of the gift described earlier by Mauss and Latour's perspective on artifacts, I argue that the mobile phone, a technological artifact, has the endowed capacity to inform, rearrange, and transvalue every aspect of society. Seeing the mobile phone through this lens fits a more recent definition of a total social fact: the mobile phone can be conceptualized as "an activity that has implications through society, in the economic, legal, political, and religious spheres" (Edgar 2002, 95). Additionally, in the mobile phone, "diverse strands of social and psychological life are woven together through what he [Mauss] comes to call 'total social facts.' A total social fact is such that it informs and organizes seemingly quite distinct practices and institutions" (Edgar 2002, 157).

This description of a total social fact seems pertinent to apply to the mobile phone in the same way as the cultural concepts of the body, the gift and reciprocity. In fact, Mauss was first to articulate the profound relationships that exist between objects and individuals, and the ways that objects are embedded in the enactment of social relationships. Building off Mauss and Latour, it would be unreasonable to consider only one dimension of any artifact or object and to treat the mobile phone as a simple communication or connectivity object. In fact, I argue that blending Mauss' total social fact concept with Latour's ANT can contribute enormously to a better understanding of co-shaping between people and technology, or human and nonhuman actants, especially by linking the micro-level of analysis (individual actors and local networks groups) with the macro-level of analysis (i.e., political economy, telecom operators, and concepts of time, space, labor, freedom, and gender). The combination of these two approaches to the analysis of objects allows me to frame the mobile phone not only as an artifact and a total social fact but as what I call a total social artifact. Conceptualized as a total social artifact, the mobile phone, as an artifact, embodies a plurality of human and nonhuman amplifying and reducing actions and activities to mediate almost every aspect of daily life, and in the process, co-influences both human action and perception; mobile phones mediate how we see and perceive the world around us and how we act within and on it (Verbeek 2005).

In other words, the mobile phone is not an object at all, but a thing in itself: "a certain gathering together of the threads of life" (Ingold 2010, 10). Within this framework of thingness, the mobile phone, made available by always-on networks of connectivity, transcends the divisions between the material and the social as well as the public and the private in a way that it is almost magical and charismatic: it is a device of expressive communication; processor of information; substitute for labor; booster of productivity and income; compressor of time and space; instrument for action; delegator of human presence and absence; and incessant rearranger and synthesizer of social, economic, political, and religious relations. It is all these things in one thing. Thus, the mobile phone's thingness, its effervescent properties, and goings-on exceed its sheer objecthood and its combined and simultaneous presence and absence have come to exert a certain weight and influence on human and nonhuman entanglements of daily life (Harvey 1990; Brown 2001). Just like the workings of the phenomenon of the Trobriand Kula ring described by Malinowski (1922) which Mauss describes as the gathering point of a whole system of prestations and counter-prestations, my argument is that the mobile phone, to use Mauss' language, "is the gathering point of many other institutions" (1990, 25). In this view, the mobile phone, a small and networked thing, brings almost everything together, grasps social life in its "perpetual state of becoming" and its fleeting moments, and influences and is influenced by the social reality of users, and in the process of this co-influencing and interplay, both humans and artifacts/things transform and transvalue almost every aspect of society.

THE GLOBAL AND LOCAL CONTEXT OF MOBILE PHONE IN MOROCCO

In the 1980s, facing negative balance of payments, severe budget deficits, and the burden of servicing international debt, Morocco subscribed to the World Bank and International Monetary Fund packages of structural adjustment policies, or the so-called Washington Consensus. This led to a fundamental shift from a state-based economy to a free-market strategy in which Morocco opened state-run monopolies to foreign competition. In the mid-1990s, there was also recognition of the importance of promoting production of high-tech industries, given their potential to create wealth, jobs, and revenue for the state. The state revamped its tariff regime and established a new legal and administrative framework for the rapid adoption of information and communication technologies (ICTs). Since that time, the Moroccan government has increased investment and adopted policies favoring the use of mobile technologies such as wireless telephony, computers, and the internet to boost business, enhance connectivity and efficiency, reduce bureaucratic red tape, make government machinery transparent, accommodate the new international requirements of E-commerce with the European Community and other trading partners, and improve the population's economic and social standards of living (see Williamson 2000; Rodrik 2006).

No other sector in the Moroccan economy has felt the effect of these economic policies greater than the telecommunications sector. In 1997–1998, Morocco's Post Office and Telecommunication Act [Loi sur la Poste et les Télécommunications], or Law 24-96, was passed, allowing for a favorable legal framework and business climate for the liberalization and privatization of the telecommunication industry. As a result of these sweeping legal reforms, the old *Poste, Télégraphe* and *Téléphone* system (PTT) was broken into two major sectors, one covering the traditional postal system (Poste Maroc), the other becoming the semi-private Maroc Télécom. At the same time, the Moroccan government established two new agencies (Agence Nationale de Réglementation des Télécommunications; and Département de la Poste, des Télécommunications et des Technologies de l'Information) whose objectives were to facilitate e-commerce; to empower the private sector as well as government ministries to use information technology; to promote technology and research parks; to infuse the educational system with new ICTs; and to provide a legal framework for the telecommunications sector (Hajji 2001). The liberalization and partial privatization of the telecommunication sector has had positive economic impacts (ITU 2001).

Morocco's telecommunications market is composed of three telecom operators. The largest being Maroc Telecom. Originally state-owned, it underwent several phases of privatization. In 2000, the French media and telecommunication group, Vivendi Universal, paid US$2.4 billion for a 35 percent stake in Maroc Telecom, which was increased to 51 percent in 2004. Today, Maroc Telecom is majority-owned by United Arab Emirates–based telecommunications operator Etisalat, which acquired all of Vivendi's shares and holds a 53 percent stake. The Moroccan state still owns 30 percent; the remaining 17 percent is listed on the stock market exchanges of Casablanca and Paris. The second-largest operator in the market is Médi Telecom, the first private operator to enter the local telecommunications industry in 2000 following the acquisition of a Global System for Mobile Communications (GSM) license in 1999 from the Moroccan government, for which they paid US$1.1 billion. These license sales were judged by market analysts, at the time, to be the most profitable transactions in the GSM markets ever in an emerging market. Like Maroc Telecom, Médi Telecom's ownership structure has undergone several adjustments. At the outset, it was owned by state-owned firm Caisse des Dépôts et des Garanties (CDG), Moroccan financial group FinanceCom, Spanish operator Telefonica, and Portugal Telecom. Since 2015, Médi Telecom has been 49 percent owned by France's Orange Telecom; the other 51 percent remains equally shared between CDG and FinanceCom. The third telecommunication company is Wana Corporate, which has operated under the brand name Inwi since its establishment in 2007. The company is owned by Morocco's Société Nationale d'Investissement (SNI or Al Mada, a large private holding company mainly owned by the Moroccan royal family), which holds a 69 percent stake. Kuwait-based Zain owns the remainder of the company.

Additionally, Morocco's political will and determination to harness the power of information technology for economic development were outlined in its national E-strategy, which was spearheaded by the Secrétariat d'État auprès du Premier Ministre chargé de la poste et des technologies des télé- communications et de l'information (Office of the Secretary of State to the prime minister responsible for Postal Services and Telecommunication and Information Technologies) (SEPTI), with ambitious goals to insert the Moroccan economy into the information and knowledge society. SEPTI, which replaced the Ministère des postes et des télécommunications (the Ministry of Posts and Telecommunication) in 1998, is responsible for design- ing, developing, and implementing national policies on ICTs (Hajji 2001; Ibahrine 2004).

Beyond simply awakening to the prospects of mobile technology as an engine of development, one of the most significant impacts of the changes in the Moroccan policy-making matrix of telecommunications deals with technological innovation and what in Morocco is known as "the new culture of the market." As one Moroccan telecommunications official told me, "By catering to the diverse needs of consumers, the new telecom operators have been successful in fostering not only a culture of 'consumer is king,' but also managed to smooth the transition to getting consumers used to the idea of new technological features and types of mobile technologies." Unlike other technologies, the mobile phone's sheer scale of adoption was driven by a series of technological and marketing innovations. First and foremost, mobile phone technology benefited from the declining cost per capability ratio asso- ciated with electronic goods as exemplified in what has come to be known as "Moore's Law," which also states that computational power doubles approximately every eighteen months. The current smartphones are far more advanced than the old low-cost feature phones with no internet connectivity or applications that I studied, but these simple feature mobile phones are the first phones for most Moroccans. By enabling communication at a distance, these mobile phones allow users to overcome time and space barriers.

An additional factor for the enormous rise of the mobile phone is the changes in the regulatory framework governing the telecommunications sector, resulting in the privatization of most of the telecommunications operators and companies. Privatization of state-owned companies created transformative innovations in business and marketing models. In Morocco, for instance, in contrast to telecommunication charges in most developed countries, only the person making the phone call pays. Moreover, mobile phone airtime is available in prepaid cards, allowing poor users to sidestep expensive contracts. For the poor laborers or smallholder farmers whose income is volatile and managing the little cash they have is critical, the prepaid card model is a major driver of mobile phone adoption and use. Even when these prepaid cards expire, they still allow customers to receive calls, providing a crucial bridge in service and marking an important business innovation in a culture once dominated by sluggish state bureaucracies.

Furthermore, as a networked device, the mobile phone comes with network effects advantages, making it more compelling for users to derive more value as more mobile phones are in use. Also, in contrast to fixed telephony, the conveniences of portability, privacy, and security of mobile phones have had a powerful pull for users. Having a mobile phone or doing whatever it takes to purchase one means wanting to be accessible at anytime and anywhere. Users are now able to coordinate their activities on the fly, and because of its networked features, the mobile phone enables and smooths multitasking and participation in instantaneous parallel activities in a plurality of places. Finally, the success of the uptake of mobile phones in Morocco owes something to the informal sector, particularly the informal markets or *joutias* in promoting and making electronic goods available and accessible to consumers en masse.

The growth in the uptake of mobiles has exceeded even the most optimistic market projections, given that Morocco is classified as a low-income country, with an annual per capita income of US$3,000. Despite the recent surge in economic growth, poverty and literacy rates are still a cause for concern, and are mirrored in a low level of human development: in 2003, Morocco was ranked 123rd out of the 189 countries and territories classified by the United Nations Human Development Index (UNDP 2003a); in 2018, it ranked 121st out of 189 countries (UNDP 2019). Approximately 50.7 percent of adults aged fifteen and above were illiterate. Women are particularly affected, with the female illiteracy rate at 62 percent; this percentage is significantly higher in rural areas. Despite slight improvement in poverty reduction, about 20 percent of the total population remains under the absolute poverty line (about $1 per day), with two-thirds of the poor found in rural areas (3.5 million, or more than 10 percent of the population). Moreover, according to the UNDP's Human Development Report (2019), about 55 percent of the rural population and 33 percent of the urban population were considered "economically vulnerable" in 2018. With an estimated population of 35.6 million, the country's agricultural economy remains dependent on rain, and adverse climatic conditions directly impact the level of rural poverty. Urban poverty is a direct consequence of unemployment, which is particularly high among the youth (up to 35.4 percent in 15- to 24-year-olds in 2018). Such indicators of high unemployment, illiteracy, and poverty contribute to insecurity and instability in rural and urban areas (UNDP 2019).

STUDY AREAS: MOHAMMEDIA AND ERRACHIDIA

This book is based on ethnographic research I conducted with urban workers and shantytown dwellers of the city of Mohammedia along the Atlantic Ocean as well as with farmers in the Ziz River Valley of the Errachidia province of southeastern Morocco. The respondents in Mohammedia consisted of informal urban daily laborers, carpenters, plumbers, electricians, female domestic workers, painters, and street vendors. They all live in the slums of Mohammedia. Mohammedia is a port city located between the country's economic capital, Casablanca, and its administrative capital, Rabat. According to the 2014 Moroccan census, the city, which had a population of only 500 people in 1914, is home to about 208,612 people (Ministère du Plan 2014). It is home to the SAMIR refinery, which produces nearly 80 percent of Morocco's refined oil. SAMIR production is delivered to 13 distribution companies and gas filling centers throughout Morocco. It also includes a thermal power plant, a fishing port, a fish market, a shipyard, and a thriving agricultural and tourism industry.

Like other Moroccan cities, Mohammedia has a serious housing shortage. The city has about 21 slums, or *bidonvilles* (oil can cities), as they are called in Morocco. These slums occupy an area of about 50 hectares with a global density of about 6 inhabitants per 100 square meters. I carried out my ethnographic work in one of the oldest slums of the city, called *bidonville* Tawreert. Tawreert came into existence in the 1930s during the period of the French Protectorate. Two major factors led to its development as a slum in the colonial period: the industrial development of the city of Mohammedia resulted in a significant need for labor and encouraged the influx of rural people from the Rhamna and Abda regions (south of Casablanca) in search of employment in industry and farming; and the policymakers of the time erected a few makeshift housing units or barracks in Tawreert near industrial and farming activities on the outskirts of the city.

Tawreert has a population of about 6,000 residents and faces problems of overcrowding and disease. The average age of heads of household is 55 years and the average household size is 6.6 persons per household or shack. Its socioeconomic conditions are characterized by high seasonality of employment, with workers divided between intermittent employees of the area's industries and a significant number of various informal activities (home services, trade, small agriculture, fishing, livestock). Self-employment and micro-entrepreneurship are pervasive in small-scale home services and trade. In Morocco, the informal sector employs approximately 40 percent of Morocco's active population, excluding agriculture.

All the slum dwellers live in substandard housing. They all live in precarious conditions where the housing stock is persistently threatening to collapse; they all live in "clandestine squatter settlements" that have been built without plans or construction permits. The slums consist of semipermanent small shacks, called *barrakas* in colloquial Moroccan Arabic, usually constructed with a mixture of sheets of corrugated metal, some adobe or cement, plastic sheeting, plywood, and cardboard. Shack structures are constantly appended, and floors are added, stacked precariously one on top of another. Shacks are divided and subdivided. The size of a shack ranges from 16 to 45 square meters (approximately 172 to 484 square feet). It is not uncommon for several families to share one shack that measures 30 square meters (approximately 323 square feet). Shack roofs are built of metal sheets and held with stones and old tires so that they will not be carried away by the wind or flash floods. Shacks are cold in winter, usually damp and leaky when it rains, and are without adequate ventilation, which, together with their metal roofs, make them extremely hot during summer. As shacks do not have piped-in water, potable water is carried in plastic cans into the shacks from public fountains. All of the shacks get their gas for cooking from pressurized containers (*buta gaz*) that residents purchase once or twice a month. Electricity is obtained through a clandestine grid connected to the city power grid. Slum dwellers suffer high degrees of respiratory illnesses (e.g., asthma), anemia, gastrointestinal illnesses, parasitic diseases, eye diseases, and epidemic skin diseases (e.g., scabies and lice infestation).

Outside the shacks, the daily environment faced by the residents is not much better. Household wastewater, rainwater, animal manure, sewage, and garbage run in open drains throughout the shantytown, producing a stench that is nauseating even for shantytown dwellers. As one electrician and slum dweller put it,

We have been living in smothering *zhaam* and *ddiq* (overcrowding and spatial constriction) and in filth (*l'wsakh*) all our lives. We live in a state of stench (*l'khanz*), we suffer from water leaks (*al-qotra*) in the roofs when it rains, and we suffer from extreme heat (*l'harara al-mofrita*) when it is hot; metal sheets are no *climatizurs* (air-conditioning) and they turn our shacks into ovens or public baths (*hammams*) in the summer.

Furthermore, deceitful political practices have also become an issue, whereby local politicians gain vote banks and office by making unrealistic promises to slum dwellers (e.g., free housing units, free electricity, and jobs). Slum dwellers are also often stigmatized by the larger Moroccan society, viewed as the source of urban problems rather than the outcome of failed political and planning decisions at the local and national levels.

Since 2004, however, the government of Morocco has been developing an anti-poverty program through the *Initiative Nationale de Développement Humain* (INDH). In Mohammedia, this program focuses on access to basic services, improvement of housing conditions, health, schooling, and employment. The government of Morocco has also been developing a slum eradication program called *Villes Sans Bidonvilles* (SVB), or Cities without Slums. The lack of housing, education, and healthcare has been identified as the main obstacle to stepping out of the vicious cycle of poverty and desperation, often a source of instability and violence (see also Bogaert 2018).

My respondents in the Ziz River Valley consisted of smallholder farmers, located in the Errachidia Province, an oasis-dominated province. According to the 2014 General Population and Housing Census, the population of Errachidia Province is 555,000, divided into 69 percent rural and 31 percent urban (Ministère du Plan 2014). The Ziz Valley population is concentrated around reliable water and in urban markets and service centers. Approximately 61 percent of the total population is employed in the agricultural sector. Population density is high in both urban and cultivated areas. The Ziz Valley's inhabitants live in fortified villages, called *ksur*, and speak Berber (Tamazight) and Arabic. These villages are large, squared structures built of adobe, sun-baked earthen bricks and stone. As a corporate settlement formation, the village cannot be separated from the palm grove, the threshing floors, the livestock grounds, the cemetery, and the olive oil press that comprise its outside organization. The palm grove is the ensemble of fields and trees owned and managed by each village. It is fragmented into a myriad of parcels crisscrossed by a meticulous network of irrigation canals and ditches.

The Ziz River Valley region is arid and part of the vast pre-Sahara region. Agricultural resources are concentrated mainly in cereal cultivation, arboriculture, and livestock. The area available for the practice of farming is 43,069 hectares, and the potential area covers 48,069 hectares making up 45,000 farming household units. The average farmer's entire holdings total less than a hectare (.86 ha), with about 65–70 percent of his total holdings under cereal cultivation (.6 ha) and the rest under alfalfa and seasonal vegetables or occupied by perennials, such as olive, fruit, and date palm trees. On the provincial level, the farming system is partitioned as follows: cereals occupy 60 percent of the farming area, barley 14 percent, alfalfa 10 percent, corn 9 percent, fava beans 4 percent, vegetable gardens 2 percent, and henna and cumin 1 percent. Over 1 million date palms and 700,000 olive trees mark the twisting, 0.5 to 10 kilometers wide Ziz Valley as it bisects the Province of Errachidia. Livestock is the third important economic aspect of the valley's agriculture, with an average of five to six head of sheep per household (Ilahiane 2004).

In summary, the potential productivity of the region is constrained by climatic conditions affecting the resilience of the valley's irrigated farming. Remoteness from major population centers, lack of transport and road infrastructure, deficient produce marketing strategies, water scarcity and its erratic variability over time and space, recurrent droughts, and frequent locust invasions have contributed to the impoverishment of the valley's environment. All these factors have, in one way or another, deferred the optimization of agricultural productivity.

RESEARCH METHODS AND BOOK ORGANIZATION

This book draws on ethnographic research on mobile phone use and economic productivity of urban street vendors, urban micro-entrepreneurs, female domestic workers, and smallholder farmers in Morocco. This study examines the way in which the mobile phone is put to economic use to create and augment business opportunities and social networks. It also investigates daily calling practices of users by analyzing incoming and outgoing logs of voice calls, the proportion of personal and business voice calls, and trends of landline phone usage. The research methods underlying this study are primarily ethnographic in nature. Employing the ethnographic practice of participant observation and structured interviews, I spent the summers of 2003, 2012, and 2016 developing a richly detailed understanding of the role of mobile phones as tools for economic development by focusing on their role among urban workers and farmers in rural Morocco. I spent time with these workers and farmers while they were involved in their trade or work activities. I played beach soccer, participated in kickboxing, and jogged with some of the urban workers, and I visited their homes multiple times. I attended Friday prayers with some of them and accompanied some of them to the public bath (*hammams*). I also went to the weekly suq or market with some of the urban workers and farmers.

The work thus combines detailed participant observation research with historical and documentary research showing the economic and social trajectories of Morocco that gave rise to the uptake and use of mobile phones. I conducted structured interviews using a questionnaire format with twenty-one farmers, nineteen female domestic workers, and thirty-two informal workers or micro-entrepreneurs (in Moroccan Arabic, they refer to themselves as *hrayfiya* or those who have a *harfa*, skill or trade) that include plumbers, carpenters, electricians, tile-laying masters, painters, skilled construction workers, and footloose or street vendors. The questionnaire consists of four parts. The first part captured standard demographic and socioeconomic characteristics of respondents (place of residence, household size, occupation, gender, age, marital status, years of education, and ethnicity). The second consists of a technology inventory of each respondent's communicative ecology (number of bicycles, number of mopeds, number of cars, number of radios, televisions, fax machines, satellite dishes, personal computers, access to the internet, mobile and landline phones, mobile phone fees, mobile phone brands, and name of mobile phone service provider). The third section obtained detailed information about the daily frequency of personal and business incoming and outgoing voice calls, the average annual income difference before and after the use of mobile phones, and the average contribution of bricolage or freelance service activities to one's annual revenue. I also recorded the type of person, or the call-partner, with whom each communication was made (family, friend, neighbor, supplier, employer, employee, or business partners), the content of that call, and its place of origin. The fourth section deals with ethnographic questions and themes on users' perception of, and attitudes toward, the transformative qualities of the mobile phone and on stories about its economic multiplier effect and expansion of business and social networks. Using a snowballing technique to recruit respondents, my study involved 72 workers and farmers using mobile phones with prepaid calling cards. Interviews were conducted in Moroccan Arabic and Tamazight (Berber). Because of low levels of education and the tradition of voice in communication exchanges, short message system (SMS) or text messaging was not used, although most respondents talked about the use of beeping (*n'beepy 'leek*, I will beep you) or "pinching" in local parlance—calling and hanging up after the first ring—their customers, employers, and suppliers.

This book is divided into five chapters plus an introduction and a conclusion. In chapter 1, I examine the informal economy of mobile phones, as a cultural domain of economic activity and entrepreneurship, by providing an intimate look into one exemplary street vendor case. In chapter 2, I am concerned with ways in which urban micro-entrepreneurs and the self-employed use the mobile phone as a tool to organize a networked work life. I examine how mobile phone use expands the productive opportunities of certain types of activities by enhancing social networks, reducing risks associated with employment seeking, and enabling *bricolage* or freelance service work, leading to income increases. I demonstrate how the use of mobile phones for *bricolage* jobs begins to *transform*, rather than simply augment the social and economic ties of micro-entrepreneurs. In chapter 3, I deal with ways in which female domestic workers use the mobile phone to expand employment opportunities. In addition, I explore ways in which the mobile phone has allowed them not only to generate more revenue but also to escape the stifling conditions of their workplace and to renegotiate the gender politics of private-domestic space. In chapter 4, I examine how and to what effects the mobile phone is used by farmers. I demonstrate how the mobile phone is a tool of organizing production and marketing of crops, leading to intensive cultivation of cash crops and higher farming incomes. I also examine ways in which the mobile phone is distinct from the delocalization properties of old technologies (i.e., the snowmobile and the truck). In chapter 5, I examine how Moroccans use mobile phones as a way of redefining issues of gender, honor, and shame, and placemaking. I show how mobile phones enable distance, becoming invaluable vehicles for inverting and suspending ordinary gender roles and placemaking practices. I also discuss how mobile phones are not just objects but are in themselves "things" and constitute multi-vectored places. In the conclusion, I summarize the findings of my study of mobile phone use in Morocco. I also highlight the limitations of my study and point out possible future paths for ethnographic research on mobile phones in the Middle East and North Africa.

Chapter 1

Street Vendors

The Mobile Phone Is a Cleaner Occupation

It is late afternoon in *joutia*, a section in the old market district of Rabat known for its wide availability of electronic goods. The term *joutia* is derived from the French words *jetez la* (throw it there) and *jetable* (throwaways). Over time, the term *joutia* entered colloquial Moroccan Arabic (*darija*); it refers to an informal trading space where thrown-away objects, secondhand things, and new items are bought, sold, and traded through the method of haggling. The narrow market street is teeming with men, women, and children, buying and selling wireless phones, computers and software, satellite dishes and televisions, video games, movies, and compact discs. Space here is a premium and overcrowding is the norm, as is pushing, shoving, and elbowing among buyers and sellers. Slowly moving throngs of people are jammed into an "L"-shaped alleyway that is perhaps 75 meters long and 3 meters wide, too narrow to accommodate even a third of them. The street vendors are called *al-farrasha*, the term *farrasha* referring to a portable piece of plastic or cloth used by vendors to display and organize goods on the ground. The place is loud and crammed with *al-farrasha*—with traders who can buy, sell, fix, or otherwise provide value to these technologies, all at prices that are a fraction in those in the modern district.

A thirty-two-year-old man sits on a mat made from a detergent carton. He is dressed in a fisherman's jacket with many pockets, a baseball cap, an "authentic" pair of "Ray-Ban" glasses, and shiny, baggy sweatpants bearing the Bouygues Telecommunications logo. He has a fanny pack around his waist and wears a relatively new pair of "Nikes." Placed carefully on a detergent box before him are dozens of new and used mobile phones. A pile of mobile phone parts lies on a plastic sheet on the ground: chargers, batteries, antennas, plastic screen protectors, leather and plastic cases, along with a new pair of "New Balance" running shoes. His toolkit, composed of a dozen screwdrivers of all sizes and shapes, a toothbrush, and a bottle of cleaning liquid, is making the rounds among his fellow street vendors. Behind him, a beautifully designed wooden box showcasing new, expensive wireless phones of varying brands hangs on the wall. "People admire the wooden box, and many people want to buy it, but I keep it to attract the eye of the strolling shopper," he tells me. "It is my *al-ishhaar,* my advertising." He offers me the box, saying, "You can have it if you want; you look like somebody who appreciates quality. You must be an `*ashaaq*, someone who loves quality, to come to *joutia. Joutia* is a treasure for those who know how to search."

He calls himself Ninja, another telling influence of globalization in this marketplace area. "Why do they call you Ninja?" I ask. "Because I know everything about what goes on here; I am very well connected; I buy and sell good quality merchandise from everywhere. I help people, and I am very honest." I was to discover there was far more to it than that.

To interact with Ninja is to be engulfed in a sea of gestures and talk, as he displays the functions and features of one of his mobile phones. He has none of the sluggishness that one might associate with the stereotypical, stuffy bazaar merchants of Moroccan cities. His eyes dart about as he talks and his movements, whether sitting or standing, are quick and sometimes abrupt. He is the very embodiment of *joutia's* agile capacity to serve as a processing conduit for global products. Global technology providers hoping to do business in emerging markets may wish to take note: this is the face of their product for a large and growing number of the world's consumers. The "official" sales staff in the gleaming shops on the other side of town, with their studied friendliness and neat attire, serve what may soon be the minority of those using their products.

Based primarily on anthropological fieldwork and considerable supporting economic and ethnographic literature, my goal is to provide an ethnographic and cultural analysis of and to introduce readers to the informal economy of mobile phones, an energetic and increasingly important phenomenon in this era of globalization, and to dispel a few myths by providing an intimate look into one exemplary case. In this age of globalization, it would be shortsighted to ignore the dynamic informal economy that makes up the bulk of the gross national product in many developing economies. And yet, the informal economy is routinely misunderstood and mythologized as "pimps, drug dealers, counterfeiters and pirates" and is particularly despised by the high-tech industry. I propose to shed more light on the world of the informal economy by focusing on the experience of one articulate, exemplary entrepreneur, who happens to operate in the highly dynamic underground economy in new, used, and black-market mobile phones.

As I investigated the world of Ninja, it became clear that one of the most interesting outcomes of globalization may be the collision of an increasing availability of nonlocally produced products with a vast pool of entrepreneurial vigor and competitive pride ready to engage it. The informal economy is more than just product counterfeiters, drug dealers, and smugglers. *Joutia* is itself an intensely interesting place. The street markets of such places as Rabat and Casablanca are renowned throughout North Africa for their thriving markets in ICTs. Here, one can find just about any high-tech product one needs, often available as soon as it is released in Europe or North America, at prices that attract buyers ranging from country farmers to urban professionals. Most importantly, *joutia* is where most Moroccans prefer to do their shopping for a wide variety of goods. As simply put by Waterbury, it is where "hundreds of thousands of adult Moroccans engage in desperate, marginal commercial activities, competing with one another for a smell, if not a taste, of the oil in the rag" (1972, 91). The place has a history and sense of importance in people's lives; the locals are comfortable there; others are decidedly not.

A growing body of business literature (i.e., Prahalad and Hammond 2002) has drawn attention to the supposedly vast potential at the so-called bottom of the pyramid. However, except for the important work of such researchers as De Soto (2000), the large and vital informal sector, accounting for the bulk of the gross domestic product (GDP) in many economies, remains mostly unexamined. This chapter is an attempt to rectify that situation.

HISTORICAL AND ECONOMIC CONTEXT OF THE INFORMAL ECONOMY

The "informal sector" is defined variously as household-based operations, self-employed individuals, and "gray market" product sellers operating without formal licensing or outside regulatory purview, including laborers or employees operating without legal contracts. It is a vast and highly diverse sector, mostly ignored by yet often penalized by policymakers. It accounts for some 50 percent of GDP of many developing economies, and 90 percent or more of all employment. The urban informal sector of Morocco, for instance, comprises about 300,000 micro-enterprises, contributes more than 15 percent of GDP, and employs more than 50 percent of the active urban population (Malaval and Shadeck 2000). Academic research and applied development studies by government and international agencies have shown that the informal sector can be among the most dynamic and sustainable sectors in both developed and developing economies (Castells and Portes 1989; Chickering and Salahdine 1991; De Soto 1987; Hart 1973; ILO 1972; King 2001; McMurray 2001; Stoller 1996).

Consider the opinion of the chief executive officer (CEO) of a Casablanca telecommunications firm that I interviewed. For him, the informal sector is underdevelopment at its worst. Street vendors and anchored shops dealers of consumer electronics

> [They] are death. They stand in the way of foreign companies, foreign invest-ments. Alcatel and Nokia wanted to establish a service center, but they could not, because of *joutia*, this bunch of amateurs. Their level of instruction is very low. They have no horizons. They are cannibals; they have education, but no expertise. They just put a piece here, and a piece there. Ninety percent of the time it does not work.

Strongly worded, perhaps, but the sentiment is not uncommon. It is, how-ever, in many ways mistaken. The trait of individualism encountered in the informal sector provides better conditions for the cultivation of rationalistic individualism characteristic of modern economic life than do the large state-run enterprises (Weber 1958; Waterbury 1972; Sen 2000). De Soto (2000), for instance, argues that the only true capitalists in many emerging economies are those operating in the informal sector. Besides its economic functions, the freedom and spontaneous culture of entrepreneurship of the informal market provide essential socioeconomic training in and preparation for globalization practices. Whether or not the multinational corporations of North America, Europe, and Asia choose to actively participate in these markets, they are affected by them.

In the 1950s and early 1960s, following the Marshall Plan's success in post-war Europe, a Western model of "economic development" affected policy and practice throughout much of the world. Conceived within the theo-retical matrix of modernization, the belief was that traditional society embed-ded in outdated modes of economic production had to give way to modern, scientific, and bureaucratic interventions in reorganizing the environment and the populace (Escobar 1995). This development philosophy fueled state-driven economic policies that focused on large-scale, capital intensive, and state-run enterprises as the tools of development. The move to bureaucratic industrialization not only displaced rural workers but created an increase in urban employment as well.

By the 1970s, its failure to deliver high standards of living was evident. Its major outcome was that it produced dual economies in the developing world: (1) the formal economy of large enterprises subsidized by the government and (2) small-scale producers (i.e., craftspersons, artisans, and small-scale agriculturalists), operating outside of the formal economy and its state-spon-sored policies and institutions.

During the 1980s and early 1990s, the disruptive impact of the Structural Adjustment Policies of the World Bank and the International Monetary Fund on the public sector led to widespread factory closures, austerity measures, and to a drastic reduction in government employment. Economic growth rates were low or often negative, and foreign direct investment was almost nonexistent (see Henry 1996; Henry and Springborg 2001). Millions of displaced workers in these large bureaucratic projects found themselves left once again to their own devices. This pattern has been repeated in numerous other countries throughout the Middle East, Africa, Asia, Latin America and can still be seen in variant form in China.

One of the most common responses has been migration. Some of Ninja's first gainful employment was beyond the borders of his own country. In the late 1980s, "Allah's way took me to Saudi Arabia where I worked as a plaster mason assistant for three years. Work in Saudi Arabia was all right, but I could not make much money. I was also far away from my family and relatives. It was a tough experience." Migrant labor, both between countries and from rural to urban environments within countries, has boomed in the past three decades. Some 175 million individuals now reside outside their country of origin, many of them for economic reasons (United Nations 2003).

For the Ninja, like many others, the move was temporary. Unwilling to put up with the distance and limited earning potential any longer, he returned to Morocco with the money he had earned in Saudi Arabia and dabbled with self-employment, first by opening a car repair shop in his neighborhood in the early 1990s. The choice was never entirely satisfactory to him, primarily because of cash flow problems. According to Ninja, "People would not pay for repairs, and even if they did, they paid very late." But cash flow was not the only thing he did not like about being a mechanic. "It was filthy work," he adds. It was not until later that decade that his real entrepreneurial opportunity presented itself.

THE MAKING OF THE INFORMAL
ECONOMY ENTREPRENEUR

Perhaps the most straightforward step in understanding the dynamics of the informal economy is gaining some insight into the abundant supply of entrepreneurs that operate there. In this regard, the journey of Ninja to the streets of *joutia* is perhaps not atypical. His is a story of experimentation and diversification, of "travel east and west," as he put it.

With the increased availability and adoption of mobile phones, it is not surprising that consumers looked to *joutia*—the very place many of them are most comfortable doing business—for their mobile technology needs rather than the formal marketplace. *Joutia* remains the traditional place of buying and selling goods for perhaps most Moroccans—and their counterparts throughout much of the world. An informal economy in ICTs has thus gained momentum in Morocco. Places such as *joutia*, mainly Darb Ghallaf *joutia* in Casablanca, have become renowned as places, according to a respondent, "where you can get anything that is anything. The latest technologies get to Casablanca before they hit the wider markets. It is the source of new products and gadgets."

The increased trade in mobile phones and associated technologies has become a safety net for a large underemployed class of ready entrepreneurs and a line of work that can be adopted if one has something to sell or trade. Entrepreneurs such as Ninja recognized that the new beneficiaries of technologies—such as artisans, farmers, plumbers, maids, and taxi drivers—would look to *joutia* as their "retail outlet" of choice. When he was introduced to mobile phone technology in 1998, Ninja abandoned his auto shop and set up his street floor mat for selling and repairing mobile phones—he recognized several beneficial opportunities in this new technology.

The primary attraction, of course, is the earning potential. "I started with ten bucks—and look where I am here. You can start with a small investment. Your capital investment does not need to be big. All you need is a good mind and a good idea to make things work," he said with an achiever's attitude. He continued, "Whatever you make, it is all profit, and there is always profit here. In the street, there are no taxes, no workers, no rent or utilities to worry about." As a mechanic, on average, he made about US$4,000 per year with "sweat and trials." One year, in the early days of the mobile phone, he made US$12,000.

Beyond the obvious economic reasons were carefully considered lifestyle choices. On multiple occasions Ninja characterized the work of mobile phone dealing as "cleaner" than the work of an auto mechanic, echoing a traditional tendency for commercial activities in the Moroccan marketplace to be hierarchically ordered, with the cleaner occupations accruing more prestige and being located closest to the main mosque (others were located on the secondary streets or outside the ramparts of the Medina). Despite the difference, the work allowed him to apply many of the same skills. It "comes natural to me because I am a mechanic." He is a *snay`i* (artisan or maker), but he knows how to fix things and fit parts together. "Repairing cars is about knowing what is wrong with the engine, missing or broken parts. I can apply that type of 'brain' to mobile phones," he says with a sense of confidence.

In addition, despite the occasional risks associated with operating out of sanctioned boundaries, he prefers the movement and freedom of the life of a footloose trader in *joutia*. His apparent preference for the unfettered lifestyle crystallizes when he compares his old, anchored profession of a mechanic with the footloose *joutia* alleyway street vendor he has become. It is not simply a matter of no overhead and no taxes. In the street, one is in the flow of the people, relationships and earning potential that comes with being in circulation. "Why don't you work for Maroc Télécom?" I asked Ninja one day after a tough, slow market day in *joutia*. He responded, "I do not want to be a government worker. It is suffocating. I want to do something I can learn from and benefit from. I want to know people. I am a people person."

Perhaps just as importantly, the advent of the mobile phone industry provided Ninja and others like him the opportunity to assert what can be viewed as a healthy competitive drive, and a platform on which to evaluate aspects of local and global product quality. It is illustrated in the following brief exchange. During one conversation, the topic of goods from "the North" was broached, which I assumed to refer to a specific geographical location. Ninja, sensing my misunderstanding, posed me a Socratic style challenge, "What is 'the North'?" I responded: "It is a geographical place, where contraband comes from . . . the Spanish enclaves." "No," replied the Ninja. "You are wrong. 'The North' is where better quality products come from." This underscores a popular belief, if not an article of faith or fact, for Moroccans: higher quality products come from "the North," outside Morocco. When talking about product quality, Ninja distinguishes between what he calls the "interior of Morocco" and "the North." The interior refers to Casablanca and "the North" means Europe, Asia, or other foreign countries.

According to Ninja, Moroccan-made goods "do not have *al-`ilem* ['science']. Moroccans do not make things or create them. Products need specific studies." Ninja's choice of classical Arabic to offer this explanation to the ethnographer is not meant merely to impress but to invoke the long history of Arab mastery of technical expertise and knowledge. Arabs in the golden age of Islam, after all, provided major contributions to the fields of mathematics, geometry, astronomy, and medicine. As Ninja talks about his business, it is clear that he is painfully aware of the loss of the historically Arab/Muslim identity of mastery over technical achievement and local autonomy in the pursuit of economic goals. The appropriation of foreign imported goods is, in many ways, as much a political as an economic statement.

This classical Arab technical mastery is distinguished from the substandard contributions of the closely held systems of production currently in place in Moroccan society. "They (Moroccan firms) are thieves. They are careless and they do not know what they are doing. Local products are corrupt. They are about tobacco, alcohol, lies and corruption." Products from "the North" associated with the smuggling circuits, he explains, are framed in terms of *d'origine* products (the real thing), while locally manufactured goods distributed throughout Morocco are considered second rate, corrupt, or simply *ordinaire*, Casablanca-made.

ECONOMIC RELATIONS AND TRADING IN *JOUTIA*

It has been more than four decades since anthropologist Clifford Geertz characterized the bazaar economy of Morocco as a "mosaic" of relationships, in which one's occupation correlated closely with a complex array of ethnic, tribal, religious, and other delineations. This complex ordering—sufficiently accessible to insiders—enabled tremendous fluidity in the conduct of commercial trade (distinctions between buyers and sellers were not made) and created various institutions in support of the traditional *suq* economy, such as the organizational framework of the caravanserai, credit arrangements (*qirad*), security agreements, Islamic Trust (*waqf*), and the Sufi brotherhood (Geertz 1979).

This mosaic has dissolved, largely as a result of many of the forces of industrialization and dislocation. The traditional urban mercantile groups, Arab and Jewish, transferred from the old city's (*medina*) bazaars to modern districts of the new cities built during the French Protectorate, especially Casablanca. Later, a large number of the Jewish population departed to Israel, France, and North America, and newcomers, such as Ninja, have arrived in the *medina*. The demise of the correlation between ethnic/religious identity and type of occupation has given rise to heterogeneous and diffuse patterns of trading arrangements; ethnicity and provenance are no longer the primary factors in providing the bazaar with a solid social matrix for its operation. Today, one is likely to buy a used foreign mobile phone from a footloose Arab on the side of the street, and then take it to the anchored Amazigh (Berber) hacker to decode it. Street vendors are far freer in their commercial activities and more open to entrepreneurial innovation than the traders of the traditional bazaar.

Yet, in many cases, Geertz's insights still hold true. In the *suq* economy, the flow of commerce is broken into a number of unrelated, face-to-face transactions. There are competitive goods and services traders; the system can absorb many people, but at the risk of turning away businessmen from economies of scale and the development of markets of petty peddling and hawking. Within this context, street vendors capitalize on opportunistic moves and tend to adopt a "*carpe diem* attitude towards commerce" (Geertz 1963, 36). Two regulatory mechanisms operative in the *suq* are a sliding price system and a carefully cultivated set of interpersonal relationships. The sliding, nonfixed, price system of commodities is about communicating economic information in an ambiguous pricing environment. In Morocco, as elsewhere in the developing world, there is a great deal of seller-buyer aggressive, competitive bargaining over the price of goods and services. Even more importantly, the bargaining sessions place primary stress between the seller and the buyer. Lacking fixed prices, brand names, advertising, and other economic indicators associated with modern firms, the buyer pits his cleverness and fund of information of the market trends against a similar strategy on the part of the seller. In fact, under some circumstances where the intention is to resell goods, one is not able to tell the buyer and the seller apart, as the seller can switch camps and become a buyer, and vice-versa. What is at issue is getting someone to buy at a desired price.

It is not as explicitly competitive as the analysis portrays it, however. In his dealings and movements, Ninja "bedazzles and enchants" buyers with information—he has all sorts of stories. He seems always to be building a montage for his scene. He is smooth; he uses this to gain the trust of shoppers and vendors. When one goes to the mobile phone store in the modern district, one will never be invited behind the counter. But in *joutia*, vendors will sit down with their customers, show them how to navigate the interface of the mobile phone, and discuss the relative merits of various technologies. Ninja and his associates spend an average of at least thirty to forty minutes with potential buyers:

> We provide free services here and there so that we can build trust; people are illiterate, and we explain to them the functions and the basics of mobile phones. All they need to know is how to use the phone for talking. That is how we do our advertisement. Good work and good words lead to social networks; and people come from all over, even people from the Moroccan Radio and Television Agency, to look for Ninja.

Joutia is also a place of ferocious competition and provides an arena for expressing one's pragmatic and shrewd values and attitudes toward competition and the general public. Keeping one's place in *joutia* is a matter of how one positions oneself vis-à-vis the crowd of rivals. As Ninja puts it,

> No one can get to me. I am smart as a Jew. A Jew is someone who will make people feel comfortable. He will talk to you and find out what you know . . . what to sell to people and how to sell it. Jewish people are not Muslims, not hypocrites, they tell you the truth. That is Islam. You see, what will create problems for you, you should leave it. Do not get into what will cause you trouble.

He also adds, "I am also *masmaar J'ha* (the "nail of J'ha") when it comes to doing trade in *joutia*." *Joutia*, according to Ninja, is also a place where self-interest, cunning, cleverness, adaptation, and lying (small and light lies) define the talk of exchanges and transactions. J'ha is a folk figure in Morocco and throughout the Arab world. He is a man of one thousand and one roles, shrewd and foolish: a trickster always deceiving the naïve, and at the same time, undoing his exploits. J'ha, in many ways, underscores the

survival values and trading practices of street vendors. A J'ha trickster story
Waterbury (1972, 94) reports capture the *joutia* mentality and attitude toward
the unsolidified nature of truth telling:

> A group of *ulema* [people of knowledge] came to J'ha one day and said to him:
> we have been told that you possess magic seeds that give you your intelligence.
>
> J'ha replied: Well, I do not want to talk about it, but it is true. I have such
> seeds.
>
> Can we obtain some? asked the *ulema*.
>
> J'ha pondered a moment: Yes, that can be arranged, but of course they do
> not come cheaply.
>
> How much? queried the *ulema*.
>
> 1,000 dirhams each.
>
> That is a lot of money, said one of the group, but I will buy at least one. He
> gave J'ha 1,000 dirhams and J'ha handed him one little seed which the man
> popped in his mouth, chewed, and swallowed. Then he erupted in anger and
> shouted at J'ha: but that's nothing but a pumpkin seed!
>
> See! said Jha, you have just eaten one seed and already you are beginning
> to learn.

As Waterbury writes, "The people have been had, but they curse their own
stupidity rather than the man who had them" (1972, 95). This tale not only
highlights the naivete of the *ulema* buyers who believe that there was such a
product as "magic seeds of intelligence," it delivers a stern warning to those
engaged in buying and selling in the marketplace. In short, successful traders in the *suq* bear all the hallmarks of master salesmen everywhere. For the
Ninja, selling and buying in *joutia* is

> About people. You really must know how to deal with them. People come from
> the "bureaucracy" (government employees); you have to know how to deal with
> them. They are pompous and selfish. But do not be afraid of them; be afraid of
> Allah, only. You have got to deal with them fairly. You have got to deal with
> them in good faith. Do not let their pompousness get in the way. If you deal this
> way, you gain rewards from Allah. Some of them are short in terms of reasoning
> or thinking. You have got to have this profession in your blood. You've got to
> have the tongue—it really brings down walls.

Sellers are constantly searching for possibilities to make deals and for
chances to build a reputation and stable clientele. Street vendors are aware of
new developments in mobile technology, and being aware of this, they see
their present and future activities as a set of related exchanges with a wide
variety of trading partners and "customers," which taken together forms the

basis for a steady flow of clients in search of new versions and features of mobile phones, or just good deals (cf. Geertz 1963, 1979). In such an environment, the sliding price mechanism provides the flexibility needed where market information is poor, market economic conditions unstable; and it mitigates these economic deficiencies by creating social capital in the forms of trust and a vast network of interpersonal relationships.

Equally important in shaping conduct in *joutia* is the role of Islam as an ethical and cultural force. In the traditional *suq* economy, the anthropological literature tells us that the most successful entrepreneurs and innovators are traders combining commercial frugality with religious principles of asceticism (Geertz 1963, 1979; Waterbury 1972). Ninja talks about ways in which Islamic ethics have shaped his attitude toward commerce.

> This is what our religion says—it is how you deal with people. It is not in the diploma you have; it is in the type of mind you have. You know, the Prophet Mohammed, peace be upon him, told us to teach our children trade and commerce. You know, the Prophet was a trader. Trade teaches you how to deal with people, teaches you character, and teaches you morality. That is what it is all about.

Furthermore, he adds:

> This is a sacred place. This spot here is my mosque. It is a gift from Allah that I can do this. The prophet gave us trade. This is a holy place. I come here to pray. This place is imbued with *baraka*, divine power. Use your tongue—give people time and advice. No need to rush them. You want to possess them. I have kids. I want to take *halal*—honestly made and lawful—money to them. I do not want to take *haram* (illicit money, or the forbidden) to them. I do not want to be one of those people who is cursed by his parents.

The capitalism of the *suq* is infused with an Islamic ideology no less than the spirit of capitalism in the West is infused with the spirit of the Protestant work ethic.

Many studies (Bohannan 1962; Bourdieu 1960; Dalton 1967; Kapchan 1996; Polanyi et al. 1957; Waterbury 1972) on peasant and traditional markets underscore the fact that traders can shield commercial ties from social relationships with partners, friends, and kin obligations; that is, in the market they treat partners, friends, and kin on a strictly business basis. This phenomenon is evident among the street vendors: "We are Muslims; we are brothers; we help each other; but at the end of the day, we do our calculations." Good-natured conflict, teasing relations, and competition among street vendors seem to maintain accountability and proper conduct of individuals. There is also the application of sanctions, both informal and formal. For instance, if street logic of mediation fails, street vendors are known to resort to the police, despite themselves operating outside the purview of the state. Individualism of traders means that they operate independently of any social pressures, make decisions entirely in terms of their own interests as they conceive them, and relate to each other through separate person-to-person deals. This does not mean that alliances or partnerships among traders are not important. The individual trader is the center of a series of linkages of composite trading coalitions and social networks.

Ninja is not alone with his wits in the competition for customers. Another social and spatial dimension of order in the street market deals with the role of what the street vendors call *al-nasaaba* or trappers. At the peak of heavy trading, usually at dusk, about thirty to forty young men form a line in the middle of the street and begin peddling all sorts of mobile phones, just a few feet from the main street vendors. The trappers dress nicely, in contraband clothing with European and American labels: Spanish soccer jerseys, "Nike" shoes, "Levis" jeans, and "Ray-Ban" sunglasses resting on their heads. They do not just sell "stuff," they embody globalization. These young men, whom Ninja calls "the unemployed young and retired cadres of Morocco," are there in the line one day, but they disappear the next.

For his part, Ninja was critical of the *al-nasaaba*: "These people just sell to make ten bucks or so to go get drunk or get high. Make their ten bucks and go. They are the 'Satan.' They dress nicely so they can gain people's trust." Like other vendors, he claims that the *al-nasaaba* are ruining the reputation of the market: "Do not buy from those guys, they will rip you off; buy from us." But in fact, behind the scenes, he and the other vendors work closely with them. The *al-nasaaba* work as loosely affiliated contractors, engaged to sell the lemons, the stuff the street vendors themselves cannot move. Even to would-be "buyers" of technology, the *al-nasaaba* are not entirely useless—they can and do provide useful information if one knows how to get it.

In addition to the often-downplayed relationships with the *al-nasaaba*, street vendors also have relationships with *joutia* brick and mortar shop-keepers. Regarding relations with the shopkeepers, Ninja says, "Yes, they are legitimate, but they are greedy. They are never satisfied with how much money they make because they must pay some to the state. As for me, I am a nomad. If I make five bucks in a day, that is great. That is the mercy of Allah." In his eyes, he is a peer of the men who own the *joutia* shops. "You have to be professional and skilled," in dealing with them. "I get parts from them; I give the store owners publicity. Their stuff is expensive, because of taxes, overhead, etc. I bring people to them, I bring them business, I bring activity." Ninja gets a discount on parts (below what ordinary consumers would pay) at the shops. The owner of the store also lets him use the electrical outlet to test chargers, mobile phones, and other elements.

Street vendors thus maintain crosscutting patterns of information sharing and services with anchored shopkeepers of *joutia*. By virtue of their place and function, street vendors appear to constitute a restless community as they move between the standing *al-nasaaba* and shopkeepers. This sense of commuting between *al-nasaaba* and shopkeepers reinforces *joutia's* agile and flexible marketing patterns in the sense that "no one in the bazaar can afford to remain immobile. It is a scrambler's life" (Geertz 1979, 187). This mobility, like his "power of the tongue," is what gives Ninja his edge. "Store owners must also respect me," he says. "They sell some of the contraband that I supply to them. I have connections with people in 'the North.'"

CONCLUSION

Ninja has become an important economic force, the face of technology, to a whole generation of consumers more at ease in the traditional marketplaces of this world. He occupies and has helped shape an ecology for the conduct of commerce quite different from that imagined by Western firms, yet one that exists in an intimate and dynamic symbiosis with Western producers. The functioning of the *joutia* stands in sharp contrast to the post-industrial model of doing business among the diffused global firms sustained and maintained by the power of the internet's integrated economic functions and institutional values (Sherry, Salvador, and Ilahiane 2003).

There is no doubt the temptation to view such a symbiosis as merely the workings of parasites and to see *joutia* as "standing in the way" of business and economic development. I argue that it may be more fruitful to investigate how the *joutia* and similar arrangements throughout the world provide opportunities and lessons for firms from the world's wealthy industrialized nations. The economic and social forces at play in *joutia*, I believe, combine to make it an experimental and innovative business model for integration into the global economy (see McMillan 2002).

As a model for innovation the informal sector has much to offer. It is a place where the exercise of economic rationality is carried out far away from the constraints and suffocating norms of bloated state bureaucracies. It is a "free trade zone," albeit informal, where economic actors trade global goods and are very familiar with global trade circuits, and fiercely compete with each other. As we have seen in this case of Morocco, historical factors have created a situation where the practice of trade in the *joutia* is shaped but no longer shackled by the weight of conservative traditions and social obligations that once characterized trade in these zones. In addition, the *joutia* and its global counterparts are places where the voices of new customers can actually be heard. Street vendors capitalize on information and knowledge funds developed within the context of the *joutia*, and they have managed to direct them toward the creation of wealth far more efficiently than the traditional bazaar economy had previously been able to achieve. Ninja stands at a vital point of intersection between those producers from "the North" and vast (but highly diverse) markets throughout the global South.

As the cost of technological goods continues to fall, more and more products are going to be affordable to a larger class of consumers. Roughly 8.3 billion of the world's people currently use a mobile phone; there are perhaps over 2 billion computers in use. Reaching beyond these current users will require innovative business strategies (cf. Prahalad and Hammond 2002; Prahalad and Hart 2002; Hammond et al. 2007). Growing numbers of consumers are no longer satisfied with generic finished products; they demand brand names and require identification with products. Informal sector entrepreneurs operate in the very marketplaces and streets that this vast population of humanity is more likely to visit for commercial trade and so provide a potential bridge between technology producers and consumers.

In sum, street vendors engage in a type of *participatory* marketing that generates feelings of identification and ownership of consumer electronic products; in fact, they are their "unpaid" sales representatives without job descriptions. "People leave my spot with their products happy and with a peaceful mind; relaxed," says Ninja. The informal economy can thus serve as a laboratory for disruptive innovations, marketing insights, and discovery. It can also provide important lessons to multinational corporations trying to integrate global and local expansion models. These lessons are very important in the competitive age of global flows of ideas, goods, and services, particularly when traditional markets are sluggish and disruptive, and the search has intensified for new and evolving market frontiers (Christensen 2000). The informal economy presents a paradox for large corporations: they are uncomfortable with it but at the same time its marketing practices are what they are trying to appropriate. Multinational corporations are changing strategies to enhance competitiveness and raise productivity by adopting more flexible, agile productive systems to soften supply-side swings, by producing services and goods upon demand, and by getting closer to clients and customers before and after delivering the goods and services. This is the sort of approach mastered by the informals—flexible and light inventory, face-to-face approach, and hypermobility; always in search of the next "in thing." The nuts and bolts for such global reorganization and integration already exist in the *joutia* and other settings, and what these informal economies lack "is not elbow but organization, not freedom but form" (Geertz 1963, 47).

Chapter 2

Urban Micro-Entrepreneurs

The Mobile Phone Is the Sixth Pillar of Islam

In this chapter, I am concerned with ways in which urban micro-entrepreneurs and the self-employed use the mobile phone to shape a networked work life. First, I examine how mobile phone use expands the productive opportunities of certain types of activities by enhancing social networks, reduces the risks associated with the search for employment, and enables *bricolage* or freelance service work, all leading to increases in income. Second, I demonstrate how the use of mobile phones for *bricolage* jobs begins to *transform*, rather than simply augment the social and economic ties of micro-entrepreneurs. This chapter is divided into five sections. The first provides a theoretical background on mobile phones; the second provides an analysis of mobile phone usage and trends of the study of micro-entrepreneurs and presents findings from the quantitative data; the third provides a descriptive analysis of the reasons behind some of the findings, discussing factors contributing to income enhancements; the fourth discusses the role of the mobile phone in entrepreneurship and the search for employment; and the final examines aspects of mobile phones and differential benefits.

THEORIZING THE MOBILE PHONE

Given the ubiquity of mobile phones, their impact, and rapid uptake worldwide, there is a growing body of literature on the mobile phone from the perspective of a variety of disciplines. As can be seen in world development reports, it has become common practice to make the distinction between information-poor and information-rich societies based partly on the availability and accessibility of such indicators as landlines, mobile phones, and the internet, especially related to the penetration rate of these technologies (ITU 2019; UNDP 2001, 2003b, 2018, 2020; World Bank 2013, 2016).

Many academic and nonacademic studies from various disciplines on mobile phones, whether funded by corporations, nongovernmental organizations, or foundations, tend to be centered on the social, rather than economic, dimensions of this new technology and take place in mostly affluent regions such as Scandinavia, North America, and Japan. These studies deal with a wide range of issues, including how mobile phones destabilize public and private boundaries and ways in which users configure personal and communal space; how technology invades public settings such as public transport, schools, and other public spheres; youth patterns of voice and text messaging to escape parental or societal monitoring mechanisms; the role of the mobile in surveillance and monitoring between adults and teens and among teens; fashion forms and consumption of the image of the mobile phone; how technology is deployed to circumvent and accommodate religious and cultural taboos of sociability; ethnographic documentation of how values and needs of end users influence device design; and unlocking the existing capabilities of mobile phones for mobile banking, e-learning, and health delivery systems (Sherry and Salvador 2001; Ling 2004, 2008; Ling and Pederson 2005; Glotz et al. 2005; Ito et al. 2005; Katz and Sugiyama 2005; Donner 2006, 2008; Goggin 2006; Kavoori and Arceneaux 2006; Maroon 2006; Bowen et al. 2008).

The economic development literature on mobile technology suggests that the availability of ICTs increases income and makes local economies more efficient (Jensen 2007; Aker 2008). One of the most celebrated case studies on the use of technology by micro-entrepreneurs is Bangladesh's Grameen Village Phone program. The program started in 2001 to demonstrate how technology could be applied to microfinance and create new business opportunities for poor borrowers that use technology. Micro-credit loans to micro-entrepreneurs, or the so-called phone ladies, originated from the Grameen Bank; Grameen Telecom provided the technology, and the Grameen Foundation and the Village Phone Program provided research and technical assistance. While there has been an explosion in mobile phone adoption around the world and some development planners have questioned the sustainability of the Village Phone Program concept in a glut of mobile phones, others have argued that the "phone ladies" have increased their average incomes substantially (Sullivan 2007). Samuel et al. (2005) examined the use of mobile phones by micro-entrepreneurs in South Africa, Tanzania, and Egypt and found that 60 percent of the surveyed micro-entrepreneurs in each country reported that the mobile phone has contributed substantially to their business profits.

Although Donner (2006) does not specifically focus on the economic productivity of mobile phones in Rwanda, he does argue that "micro-entrepreneurs use their mobile phones to increase the frequency of their contact with friends, family, and existing business contacts and to facilitate new contacts with business partners, suppliers, and customers" (2006, 14). On the other hand, Molony (2008) found that mobile telephony plays a limited role in the economic and social lives of Tanzanian workers, as they prefer face-to-face communications. He writes, "While mobile phones can help forge new relationships within the market, they play little part in strengthening current relationships" (2008, 654).

From an urban planning perspective, Townsend (2000) states that the use of mobile communications is constantly, and in a chaotic fashion, reconfiguring the way in which urbanites deal with spatial and temporal constraints of the urban built environment and function. He writes,

> The mobile might lead to a dramatic increase in the size of the city, not necessarily in a physical sense, but in terms of activity and productivity. No massive new physical infrastructure will emerge; rather it is the intensification of urban activity, the speeding up of urban metabolism. (2000, 14)

Anthropological research on the economic impacts of the use of information technology is slowly growing. Horst and Miller carried out ethnographic research on income-generating opportunities related to cell phone use in Jamaica. They write that "the phone is used much less among low-income Jamaicans in connection with either jobs or entrepreneurship than we anticipated" (2005, 761). They point out that the primary function of the mobile phone for Jamaicans is to "link up," referring to ways in which Jamaicans keep an active log of personal and kinship contacts on their phone to be tapped into when social and economic needs arise. The "link-up" function can include parents facilitating the participation of emigrants and "foreigners" in the daily lives of their children; the regular transfer of remittances within as well as into Jamaica; explorations of transnational marriage; and pursuit of sexual relations.

What is missing in much of this work is a detailed, empirical focus on the economic and social impact of the mobile phone on individual users, specifically its impact on user's incomes and livelihoods. Choices made by urban poor users about technology are negotiated in distinctive ways, laden with power differentials and the expressed goal to escape the grinding poverty of slum dwelling, irregular employment, and a poor and unpredictable urban transport system. Many among those who informed my study see the world as consisting of those who are poor and submissive with limited windows of economic mobility and those who are rich and domineering with unlimited opportunities. Their expressed goal is to eventually leave the world of slum living and poverty behind and make inroads into the proverbial other side of the tracks. One's choice of technology investment must be seen to directly support this aspiration. The mobile phone is not chosen simply for leisure, but with economic utility in mind.

My evidence suggests that mobile phones make a financial difference in the incomes and livelihoods of users, not simply by virtue of the ability of the mobile to connect people regardless of time and place but also by virtue of its use to both intensify and extend local and nonlocal forms of communication within social and economic networks. In so doing, users have been able to deploy the mobile to create and sustain new pockets of entrepreneurship and special social ties, enabling them to piece together economic opportunities that would otherwise be impossible.

STUDY FINDINGS

This chapter draws on ethnographic research on mobile phone use and economic productivity among skilled and semi-skilled urban micro-entrepreneurs, centered in a shantytown in the city of Mohammedia near Casablanca, Morocco. This chapter examines the way in which the mobile phone is put to economic use to create and augment business opportunities and social networks. In addition to the ethnographic practice of participant observation, I conducted structured interviews using a questionnaire format with thirty-two informal micro-entrepreneurs (in colloquial Moroccan Arabic, they refer to themselves as *hrayfiya* or those who have a *harfa*, a skill or trade) that include plumbers, carpenters, electricians, tile-laying masters, painters, and skilled construction workers.

The average age of the interviewees is thirty-one years. Most have been schooled in Quranic school or public educational institutions: 12.5 percent are illiterate, 3.1 percent attended Quranic school, 59.4 percent attended primary school, 25 percent attended secondary school, and none attended postsecondary school or university. The average number of years of education is 5.5 years. In terms of household conjugal status and size, 38 percent were married, 53 percent were single, and 9 percent were divorced, with an average of 3.5 persons per household. The occupational profiles of respondents included plumbers (21.9 percent), carpenters (9.4 percent), tile-laying masters (18.6 percent), skilled construction workers (12.4 percent), electricians (15.5 percent), and painters (21.9 percent).

To have a comprehensive understanding of the context of technology in the lives of the respondents, I collected information on the presence of modes and means of social contact and media use other than the mobile phone. In terms of ownership of traditional forms of mass media and mobility: the mean number of bicycles per respondent surveyed was 1.5; mopeds stood at 1.3; video players stood at 1.03; radios at 1.5; television sets at 1.25; and satellite dishes at 1.5. For comparison, the average number of mobile phones per respondent is 1.3, and the number of mobile phones acquired over the past five years was 3.0. While none owns a personal computer and access to the internet is insignificant, all respondents had mobile phones, and only one respondent had a complementary landline, which was at work.

Quantitative evidence on usage patterns of mobile phones for personal and business calls shows a monthly mean of 38.06 personal calls and 102 business calls per respondent. The analysis also shows that respondents spend a monthly average of 130 Moroccan dirhams (US$13) on prepaid calling cards for their mobile phones, and about 77 Moroccan dirhams (US$7) on public pay phones (*téléboutique*). On average, respondents spend about 4.8 percent of their monthly income on telecommunication fees; 3.8 percent on prepaid calling cards for their mobile phones, and 1 percent on public phones. To assess the economic impact of the mobile phone on users' income and on shaping respondent social networks, I examined the pre- and post-mobile average income of the respondents. The analysis indicates that mobile phone use has resulted in an increase of 56 percent in users' incomes.

MAKING SENSE OF MOBILE PHONE USE

What were the causes of this considerable increase in income? As my analysis suggests, there are several contributing factors. In addition to the financially rewarding and lucrative *bricolage* jobs brought by the mobile phone, the respondents emphasized its "help" in expanding the size and scale of their operations and recognized the significant economic contributions of the mobile phone to the bottom line of their businesses. One plumber, for instance, said that "the mobile gets one out of his circle and into other circles."

Goodman (2005) argues that mobile phones in South Africa and Tanzania are being used more often to sustain existing strong social ties, especially family, than for supporting or building other weaker and distant ties. Donner (2006) reports that Rwandan micro-entrepreneurs use the mobile phone as a "job telephone" and as a tool to increase the frequency of their contacts with friends, family, and existing business contacts and to facilitate new contacts and leads with business partners, suppliers, and customers. While there is a potential economic impact of the mobile phone, he points out that the device is mostly put to use within the immediate and inclusive networks. Granovetter (1973) has argued that when seeking jobs or political allies, the "weak ties" that bind individuals to distant acquaintances that move in different circles are actually more valuable than the "strong ties" that link one to intimate friends or relatives who operate in the same social and economic niche. This seemed to hold true among my contacts. Everyone had a story about how the mobile phone is a means of staying in touch (*tawassul*) even with distant contacts, and this staying-in-communication is vital to knowing what is happening in the social and economic scenes and for leads to additional employment opportunities. One electrician said,

> When I met Youssef, we worked on a job together in Meknes [210 kilometers (132 miles) from Mohammedia]. He was a nice guy, but after the end of the job, the relationship would have been over. Now the phone allows us to keep in touch. I have him (meaning his number) in my phone and he has me in his.

A plumber told me, "One week I had nothing to do. I called my friend in Fez. He knows I am a good worker and he told me that there is work."

At the same time, on the local level, the mobile phone appears to augment relationships of the users with their families and with work friends. Both locally and nonlocally, it provides an additional channel by which they extend relationships in time, refresh local relationships, and slow the decay rate of external relationships. This intensification of contact seems to offer potential for economic productivity. Such intensification may ultimately depend on a mixture of place-based and interest-based networks.

Consider the example of one plumber who also owns a brick and mortar plumbing store and is the only respondent in the surveyed sample with a landline phone subscription. This plumber exists at the hub of an entire network of carpenters, plumbers, electricians, painters, masons, roofers, tile-makers, maids, and others. The mobile phone, as per Townsend's insight (2000), enables the plumber and his contacts to rapidly mobilize in response to a need or opportunity. Note, however, that the effectiveness of the mobile network rests on a somewhat more complex mix of placed-based and interest-based interactions where the "work" of preparing this network of providers is carried out.

The plumber himself occupies a privileged position within the network by virtue of his modest physical storefront. It represents a known "first stop" for people who do not know where else to turn for help with their household repairs, building plans, or improvement needs. There are no Yellow Pages; people come to him. The plumber keeps and manages a directory, or *kunash*, listing names and mobile phone numbers of *hrayfiya* (skilled laborers). He is also able to tell customers about the location and the availability of any of his associates; in a sense he is in the business of arranging and matching service seekers with service providers. His store serves as a physical anchor, a touch point into a trusted, accountable network of providers. The very presence of the store communicates to customers the plumber's willing accountability in this system of referrals. "Trust me," his store says, "I will find you the right person. And you know where to find me if it turns out bad."

The plumber's own network of relations and associates, in turn, is built up through a cluster of place-based and interest-based interactions—at the café, the soccer field, the mosque, the job site—where working relationships and bonds of trust are formed, where information about opportunities is exchanged, along with verbal banter and teasing, discussions about the relative merits of techniques and tools, and discussions about other workers and various clients. This cluster of networks and interactions provide a kind of platform on which the plumber and many members of his social network assemble and pursue the relations that govern their modest economic livelihood.

Putnam (2000) discusses the dimensions of social capital forms and builds on Gittel and Vidal's (1998) differentiation between bonding (local) and bridging (external). Putnam (2000, 13) argues that while bonding social capital shores up narrow and local interests, bridging social capital can result in extensive and broader forms of reciprocity and networking. To paraphrase Putnam, the *passe-partout* properties (i.e., time and space compression) of the mobile phone provide a "sociological WD-40" to recalibrate and align different yet complementary sources of employment such as shopkeepers, café shops, worker friends, and neighbors. The mobile phone succeeds in reinforcing and speeding up hectic urban interactions, and at the same time, infusing disjointed networks and activities into coherent sets of activities (Townsend 2000). Seen through this lens, the mobile phone simultaneously bonds and bridges users along and across social and economic dimensions, and this is perhaps the "secret" of its power to break down the boundary between social and economic spheres (see also Donner 2009).

The example of the plumber's network suggests that new technologies do not necessarily succeed by simply displacing other modes of communication. The plumber's modest storefront, now augmented with the mobile phone, represents the way that new technologies succeed by adding to existing systems and networks. The traditional means of connectivity and mobility such as bicycles, mopeds, and public transportation also contribute to the health of social networks and are obviously all necessary for physically getting to job locations. The mobile provides the plumber's customer an instant connection into a network of trusted and "vouched-for" contacts. For the plumber the mobile provides a chance to make another sale (he becomes the supplier to the contacted workman). The mobile also provides the opportunity to enhance his *social capital*—his prestige within the network and stronger reciprocal bonds with those whom he has referred. For the lucky recipient of the plumber's call, it provides a chance for much desired work. Mobile phones thus enhance, rather than displace, other places in the network, and the "work" of relationship building across these other places pays off with the phone call. The network of the storefront/work site/mosque/football pitch/café, and the network of associates developed there, and the work carried on at these places, is rendered more valuable by the presence of the mobile phone. As Harper cogently puts it, "The mobile is a kind of *invigorating* of social relations" (2003, 194).

A major effect of this easier access to social networks is an upgraded ability to engage in what my contacts called *bricolage*, augmenting one's income by engaging in much more ad hoc, supplemental labor. For the skilled laborers I observed and interviewed, *bricolage* jobs include emergency or routine home repairs and improvements, usually occurring after normal work hours. Such projects ranged considerably in scope, from fixing a leaking water pipe, to installing water heaters, to major bathroom renovation projects. My data also demonstrates that *bricolage* accounts for 31 percent of a respondent's monthly income. Additionally, for many in my sample, the mobile enabled them to serve multiple households, allowing them to be more fluid in their location and engagement of work.

EMPLOYMENT SEARCH AND THE
ENTREPRENEURIAL SPIRIT

When asked about reasons for purchasing a mobile phone, one carpenter looked at me for a minute, shook his head, and released a controlled, short laugh, only to declare in no uncertain terms,

> The mobile is very important for the *hrayfiya* community in terms of communication inside and outside Mohammedia; you are here and there at the same time. The mobile brings work and moves you forward here or anywhere else where jobs are available; that is the secret of the mobile.

One plumber simply said,

> It is my lifeline to earning my bread and to keeping in touch with my family and friends here and in other places; in addition, you must get one as employers and potential employers always ask for a mobile phone number; with it I have increased my economic earnings.

He continued with a serious face and a question, "How many pillars are there in Islam?" I responded, "five pillars," referring to the obligatory duties that every Muslim must practice. The plumber responded with poise, "Yes. There are five pillars, and the mobile phone is the sixth pillar of Islam. Now, you know the importance and meaning *(ma'na)* of the mobile in our daily lives!" Another laborer added,

> If you want to pray, you need to pray in the direction of Mecca *(qibla)*. It is the same with the mobile. If you want work wherever it is, you need the mobile. There is no prayer without *qibla* and there is no work, except on rare occasions, without the mobile! Do you get it now? Additionally, if you do not pray, you have no religion, you have no rite. And if you do not have a topped-up prepaid card in your mobile, you do not have a religion.

What is moving about these statements is the fact that the workers consider having a mobile phone so meaningful as to view it as an additional pillar to the five pillars of Islam. The five pillars are mandatory rituals and duties (except for pilgrimage) and are commandments that every Muslim must practice. One must profess *al-shahadah*, one must perform the five daily prayers, one must perform almsgiving, one must fast the month of Ramadan, and, if able, one must take a pilgrimage to Mecca. These are the practices that define what it means to be Muslim. The sixth pillar, or the mobile phone in this conversation, is metaphorically seen as an order or a commandment. The necessity of doing what it takes to acquire a mobile phone underscores the fact that one cannot go about one's daily business and rituals without it; it is an obligatory duty that brings job opportunities/possibilities and anchors one's identity, just as the five pillars of Islam bestow identity and meaning to one's religious life.

One of the benefits of the mobile phone is that it lowers the cost of finding work. Most respondents draw circles—increasingly large circles—to illustrate the "serious" economic benefits associated with the mobile. The mobile phone has enlarged the radius of distance *hrayfiya* travel to find work. One plumber traveled from Mohammedia all the way to the city of Dakhla (2,000 kilometers or 1,243 miles away) where a company had a contract to build schools. One of the employees who used to work for the company (a plumber) was let go, but the company said, "We'll call you if we need you." That plumber then received the call and called his plumber friend. Both of these plumbers now had work in a faraway place; prior to the arrival of the mobile phone, this opportunity likely would not have presented itself. The mobile has brought convenience for both the worker and the hiring party; both sides are incentivized. This is particularly important in places where these construction companies do not want to maintain a regular workforce. They keep a virtual workforce upon which they can rely when they need workers, which saves them money. The notion is, "I keep you in my range!" This small amount of connectivity appears to be driving major economic trends. It optimizes both the time of both the laborer and the hiring company because they now have access to a more fluid and dynamic workforce.

Consider the situation of one tile-laying master. He is about 54 years of age and has been in the tile-laying business for as long as he can remember. One of his dreams was to scale up his tile business operation and to "export" his skills outside of his home town, Mohammedia, in order to make more money. Although he tried to do so, he failed many times; he blames his failures on time constraints and costs associated with transport, supervision efforts, and communication. Only with the emergence of the mobile phone could the tile master envision the idea of working "here and there." With a mobile phone in hand, coupled with vast experience in tile work and a good reputation with people, the tile master finally became a contractor and has three work crews in multiple sites in Mohammedia and Rabat. The mobile phone has enlarged the circle of opportunity for the tile-laying master and the mobile phone, in his opinion,

> is like a saint to whom you go to solve your problems and concerns, and it works miracles for you. It is a blessing that I can sit here in Mohammedia and check on my associates and get information on their progress. There is nothing like it and the money is good. Before I only worked around here; now we are ready to go to your house to put in some good Moroccan tile if you wish.

The *hrayfiya* in this study, like the tile master, have exploited the coordination and organization proficiencies of the mobile phone. Of the surveyed sample, 25 percent of respondents have successfully harnessed the portability asset of the mobile and created micro-enterprises employing between four and nineteen workers in and out of town. I calculated that in my sample one mobile phone creates about 8.62 jobs and travels an average distance of 405 kilometers (250 miles). All the surveyed respondents, whether they liked or disliked mobile phones, stressed the importance of owning a mobile phone, and they also emphasized the fact that by the mere fact of having one, one has access to real and potential job opportunities. For these reasons, many respondents said that they did everything they could, even borrowing money from relatives and friends, to buy a mobile phone.

MOBILE PHONES AND DIFFERENTIAL BENEFITS

While micro-entrepreneurs are aware of its economic benefits and entrepreneurial drive, there were undeniable perceived downsides of mobile phone access and use in terms of power relationships and differential benefits. The mobile phone is not, as some literature has suggested (i.e., Ling and Pederson

2005; Glotz et al. 2005; Ito et al. 2005a; Katz and Sugiyama 2000), a marker of social status in and of itself. This was reflected by the people I encountered. One carpenter, when asked about the social and economic inequality implications of mobile phone use, said,

> A good reputation, trust, and seriousness are what distinguish one skilled laborer from another. Now, with the mobile those who do a good job and have good social relations and work with good intentions tend to get ahead of others. The mobile phone alone is not enough. One has to be skilled in his trade and must know how to deal with people. Beware of those who use the mobile phone as a status symbol and pretend to be good skilled workers. Some get away with it but not for long, and they are back in the laborers' stand, under the sun!

A laborer with a mobile phone but with no connections or without a good work reputation finds himself or herself at an economic disadvantage. The mobile phone perhaps best enhances the earning potential of individuals who already have a comparative advantage of some sort, like a network, a good reputation, or a professional skill or trade. While the store owner increases his or her power and status by virtue of his or her multistranded network of social relations and business contacts and by having a physical location, the laborers at the day laborer stand (*al-mawqaf*) do not stand out as individual contributors in a network of providers. Consumers who might once have gone to the day laborer stand (and take their chances with the quality of labor and reliability) can now go to the plumber's shop with a specific request and get connected with the plumber's network of service providers, which have been vetted by the plumber. The less differentiated and less connected day laborers have suffered.

Among my contacts, there were also respondents who saw the always-on mobile phones as a means of control and a source of annoyance and "headaches." One master builder, for example, expressed this sentiment clearly:

> The mobile phone gives more power to the people who have financial means. This mobile phone means that I never have a religious holiday or sleep well. The employer, a bank manager in this case, in his pajamas in his villa, can call or summon me to fix a problem on the Day of Sacrifice. What is there to be liked about the mobile?

The mobile also affects the productivity of labor, to the advantage of the employer. The master builder explained,

> In the old days, when we ran out of cement and iron rebar, work would stop; we would have some down time. Now, the boss tells me that as soon as we are

running low on supplies, to beep him, and he will make sure that new supplies are purchased from the market and delivered to the work site on time. So, we are now working harder, and getting paid for fewer hours.

Another aspect that seems to pain the master builder and his carpenter associate is the culture of surveillance and intimidation that the real or imagined presence of the mobile phone brings about in users:

> You never know when the boss is watching you. Is he in his villa? Is he on the road? Is he hiding just around the corner in his car or behind that little hill? He might call you from somewhere just near the worksite. Nobody knows; only Allah knows where he might be.

I replied, "But the mobile helps you to be accessed. As a master builder, you can have multiple sites going and make more money." "I do not care about that. I do not want that," the master builder said forcefully. Before the mobile phone, he had a good quality of life because he was at the center of an "easygoing network." Now he is forced to hustle and speed up work tasks, and he cannot find tranquility. He goes on to say that "even if I did not buy a mobile phone, the employer would buy me one. The mobile phone works for the people with means and money, not for us poor people." He is subsidizing the employer, in a way, because with the mobile phone the employer is able to "parallelize" his own operations, by enabling him to remotely supervise the building site while also concentrating on his other business. Even with the mobile phone, the employer will make a couple of visits per day to the site to see the progress on the house and check on the master builder and his workers.

One more thing that troubles our master builder in relation to his mobile phone, he says, resides in the fact that "the mobile phone gathers it all. In it there is the house, places of work, the marketplace, the mosque, family problems, migraines, and surveillance from afar." Just as the mobile reduces the costs and risks associated with travel to job sites and personal networking, so it enables greater flexibility in labor selection (and hence, less commitment to any individual worker), easier surveillance, and parallelization of work. Such benefits clearly favor those who are economically well off. In sum, as one sociologist turned public servant told me,

> The mobile phone fits nicely in our culture and the Moroccan way of doing business. Employers use the mobile phone to yell at their workers: "Did you do this?" "Did you take care of this?" "Why didn't you do this? Are you trying to ruin me?" They never say please or thank you. It is part of the culture of fear and intimidation.

In fact, even on the job site, the master builder reproduces some traits of this type of business culture and must assert his own dominance over the laborers. He must keep his reputation as a master builder. You do not question him, but if you do not like him, you can always move on. Clearly, the mobile has not reformed all aspects of labor relations.

CONCLUSION

In the aforementioned discussion, I document the use and importance of mobile phones to micro-entrepreneurs, low-income users, and the self-employed in urban Morocco. I also demonstrate ways in which mobile phone users harness the power of connectivity to generate income and to scale up business operations and activities. Based on my empirical findings, access to telecommunications boosts incomes and creates economic opportunities.

I demonstrate how the use of mobile phones begins to transform and augment, rather than simply reinforce, business operations and social relations. Among my contacts, the mobile phone enabled a greater degree of agency among individuals in identifying and capitalizing on work opportunities by enhancing their ability to both nurture and tap into social networks more fluidly. This reduces risks, enables bricolage, and enhances social standing for the skilled workers I observed. For these micro-entrepreneurs, the distinguishing characteristics appear to be the innovation of mobile phones and the audacious exploitation of economic opportunities that arise. The innovations made possible by mobile phones enabled urban workers who previously lacked efficient means of communication to form efficient and viable micro-enterprises. Furthermore, despite the observation that mobile phones offered differential benefits depending on one's location in a social network, most did not regard the mobile as exclusionary and divisive.

Chapter 3

Female Domestic Workers

The Mobile Phone Is like a Saint

In this chapter, I focus on how the mobile phone is used by female domestic workers or maids to create new economic opportunities and redefine traditional social obligations and bonds in Morocco. I argue that mobile phone use by maids has resulted in higher revenues by widening the circle of economic activity and by facilitating supplementary informal income-generating opportunities. I also argue that the mobile phone is changing the experience of social and business networking and, by extension, individual agency and freedom.

This chapter is divided into five sections. The first discusses employment search approaches used by maids before the arrival of the mobile phone; the second describes the social context of the phenomenon of female domestic workers; the third presents the study findings; the fourth provides a descriptive analysis of the reasons behind some of the economic effects from the quantitative survey data, discussing both factors contributing to income enhancement and ways in which this new technology has been rendered charismatic; and the fifth examines how mobile phones mediate new forms of sociality and control over women.

EMPLOYMENT SEARCH BEFORE THE MOBILE PHONE

While it is difficult to provide exact figures on domestic household labor at the national level, especially regarding domestic female workers, it is widely accepted that it is a significant part of the national household economy (Lahlou n.d.; Montgomery 2019). During my interviews and conversations with them, maids used the French term *bonne* to describe their household labor activities and tasks. The term *bonne*, or *khaddamah* in colloquial

Moroccan Arabic, refers to women or young girls who work as domestic workers in homes other than their own, and are paid a monthly salary. The daily domestic tasks and chores performed by maids include running errands and going to the marketplace; cooking; taking care of children; washing and ironing clothes; sweeping and scrubbing floors; and doing the big cleaning or the "*grand ménage*" of the house.

When asked about ways in which they find work, the maids identified three methods through which they find potential employers. The first one involves the use of "semi-professional" middlemen or women, known in Morocco as *samsar* (masculine) and *samsara* (feminine). The *samsar(a)* works as a broker between potential employers and maids. He or she occupies a vague professional space in the sense that the *samsar(a)* profession is oftentimes an add-on source of extra income to supplement other economic activities, and as such falls outside the purview of the state and its bureaucracy. The *samsar(a)* locates maids, places them in homes, and earns a one-time fee for the service from the employer. Due to the *samsar(a)*'s centrality in these transactions, he or she is approached by both employers seeking maids and parents searching for work for their daughters. The *samsaras*, I was told,

> know who is who and who is looking for whom and for what. The *samsaras* know this place and they know people in rural areas. Since they are also involved in house hunting and rental transactions, they really have the keys [figuratively] to the ins and outs of the neighborhood and its surroundings.

Furthermore, once maids use the services of the *samsar(a)*, the relationship between the *samsar(a)* and the maid develops into an important channel of communication with regard to identifying better jobs with better pay and kinder employers. In turn, by staying in touch with maids, the *samsar(a)* can make money each time he or she identifies a new place of work for a maid. Because of the economic benefit they stand to gain from each placement, *samsaras* often encourage maids to leave their jobs, place them in new homes, and, in the process, manage to undercut the development of long-term relationships between employers, maids, and their parents. Seen through this financial calculus, maids come to represent valuable assets in the competing interest and demands of parents, *samsaras*, and employers.

The second method that maids use for seeking daily or short-term employment is to travel to and appear in person at the informal labor station and service delivery platform for day laborers, usually located near the marketplace. The labor station, called *al-mawqaf*, refers to the place where skilled and semi-skilled laborers congregate informally as they wait to connect with employers. The labor station, according to one maid, "is not my preferred place to look for work. It is not safe, and it is far away from my neighborhood. Besides, most employers do not trust the labor stand's laborers." Lastly, maids obtain employment through building good relationships with neighborhood shopkeepers and through investing time to get to know and network with other maids, all of which leads to referrals within these connections. Since the advent of mobile phones, maids have developed the practice of leaving their mobile phone numbers with shopkeepers and watchmen who guard villas and houses of the upper and middle class in the hope of being called on for potential employment opportunities.

THE SOCIAL CONTEXT OF FEMALE
DOMESTIC WORKERS

Although there has been a growing body of literature on the *petites bonnes* or "young little maids" within the context of child labor and human rights since the 1990s (Sommerfelt 2001; Lahlou n.d.), there is little research about adult maids and ways in which they have employed the communicative reach of mobile phones to enhance their social and economic conditions. In her seminal article on the life and aspirations of a Moroccan maid, Mernissi (1982) captures the marginality and subordination that maids are made to feel and occupy in the domestic and public spaces. She writes, "You know that in our country (Morocco), to be a maid is the lowest of jobs; nobody respects you. Nobody wants to go with a maid or have a friendship with her. Moroccans despise maids and ridicule them. They would laugh at you if you told them you were a maid" (1982a, 17). She goes on to discuss the phenomenon of maids and underscores the power dynamics and the asymmetrical and exploitative relations between urban and literate upper- and middle-class women and poor and illiterate rural women. Mernissi writes,

> The appearance of a group of women with diplomas and paying jobs has been accompanied by the appearance of another group just as visible and statistically important—that of maids . . . in the city the rural origins of maids is an instance in which the rural is held to be inferior to the urban, and this with regards to expertise. The maids in the city are the incarnation of the degradation of manual labor identified as primitive and nonproductive. They are paid less than the minimum wage and have the protection of neither social security nor labor unions. Like the peasant women who bore them, they suffer every day in the city the contempt with which the city has traditionally regarded the countryside in North African history. (1982b, 100)

While Mernissi's discussion of maids provides a structural analysis for understanding the phenomenon of domestic workers, Kapchan (1996) describes

ways in which maids are portrayed within their respective homes of employment and within the larger society. Maids, she argues, are described as thieves,
liars, subordinates, "daughters of sin," and, most importantly, they embody
imminent threats to the cohesion and viability of the household unit. She states,

> Maids are not only portrayed as embodying dirt, but . . . they are morally dirty
> and threaten to contaminate the family they work for . . . not only does the maid
> transgress sexual norms, but she is feared as someone without ethics. Because
> of her symbolic marginality in the home and her centrality in the marketplace,
> the maid is always suspect. She is often portrayed as a thief. . . . They are *bnat
> l'hram*, the daughters of sin, presenting an explicit sexual threat to the women
> of the house. (Kapchan 1996, 230, 232)

The aforementioned quotes demonstrate the difficult social and economic
predicament of maids and the restrictions imposed on them. The maids interviewed in this study highlighted similar concerns such as degradation, shame,
insecurity, embarrassment, and harsh treatment by employers and *samsaras*
as well as their parents. Khadija, a thirty-five-year-old maid and a shantytown
dweller, has been working for almost thirteen years as a maid and supports
eight of her siblings on a monthly salary of about 700 dirhams (US$70).
Khadija spoke about the low status and associated traits allocated to maids in
Moroccan society. With a sense of relief and sadness in her voice, she said,

> *Al-khaddama* [maid] has no *qimah* [value]. They make us wear long pajamas,
> not pants [meaning they wear traditional Moroccan maid attire and are not per-
> mitted to wear jeans, or modern style pants]. They make us appear that we are
> maids. We always wear *tabliya* [apron]. Maids ride in the back of the car, eat
> in the kitchen, they cannot feel like they are at home, and they cannot go out.
> Television is not an option and some employers do not let maids watch TV or
> use the phone or even recharge the battery of their mobile phones due to the cost
> of electricity and *katyyah addaw* or causing a power outage.

Karima, who refers to herself as a veteran maid and as someone who is
aware of what society thinks of her profession and the stigma of being a maid,
highlights additional difficulties encountered in this line of work. She also
speaks of those maids who serve as a source of income for parents who care
only about money. In a forceful manner, she voiced:

> Every month parents from the *bled* [countryside] come to collect a portion of
> the salary. You are lucky if you go out once every two weeks. They [employers]
> want to own you, (*n'shaduha n'wartuha makaynsh al-weekend*). Some maids, if
> they protest their situation and leave, are accused of theft. Maids also run errands

in bare feet, so they do not run away. If they do run away, they are either beaten with a stick/belt or burned. Also, the stigma of being a *khaddama* is a major problem for future [marriage] prospects. *Anti ghir (kunti) khaddama*: you are or were only a maid. You cannot propose, you can only take orders. This is *saytara 'ala al-bnat* [domination over girls], no conscientiousness (*al-damir*) and no education. Parents of rural girls tell employers to not let their daughters go out. *Al-bnat* [girls] go home twice a year or once a year (on the Day of Sacrifice each year). *Al-khaddama* talks from the balcony or the window and does not go out.

In the aforementioned account, Karima tells of loneliness, isolation, vulnerability, and desperate conditions in which maids find themselves trapped and she speaks to various ways in which they are dominated by employers. What is noteworthy is that where maids are made to feel like a piece of property or a commodity, it seems that their sole way of escaping such a suffocating and repressive space is through the occasional use of the balcony and the window to see and be seen by the outside world. Hence, in addition to intermittent but short contacts with shopkeepers and villa guards, the balcony and the window have come to constitute the main channels through which maids can communicate their humanity to the rest of society.

All the maids I spoke with differentiate between good and bad work experiences. All the maids concur that working for foreigners, especially the French, is better than working for Moroccan upper- and middle-class families. Jamila said,

European employers pay better than *al-'arab* [Moroccans] or the Arabs. They give value to *al-khaddama*. For Moroccans, *al-khaddama* is not a person of honor (*mashi insanna sharifah*). They mistreat her as if she was not earning her keep on her own; this is *al-hogra* or contempt, so much of which is displayed before your eyes. *La Bonne*, for the French, is a human being and not an animal. She eats with them at the table and they think of her in *Bonne Année* (New Year). They offer her *Eid* money, sometimes buy her the *Eid* ram, pay her overtime, and if she finishes her work late at night, the French employer gives her a lift to her dwelling in the shantytown. There is a big difference between *al-goor* [Europeans] and *al-mgharbah* [Moroccans].

Jamila clearly distinguishes between French and Moroccan families in their care for their maids. Maids feel that social and economic differentiation is more pronounced in the upper- and middle-class Moroccan homes than in French ones. All the maids stressed the firm boundaries between maids and the family members of Moroccan employers to the extent that maids are made to feel like subhumans or low creatures. While French employers are portrayed as kind, charitable, and considerate, maids emphasize that Moroccan employers show them contempt, or what they call *al-hogra*: an attitude expressing overt hatred and derision as if to remind them at every moment of their low value and status in the chain of humanity. It is quite revealing to note the explicit use of the term *al-hogra* by maids in this context (*al-ihtiqar* in Arabic). The term *al-hogra*, although used mostly in the political arena, refers to a set of ideas ranging from injustice and corruption, to real and symbolic violence, through abuse and disenfranchisement, to plain hatred and condescension. From the maids' point of view, not only does the *al-hogra* concept reveal their economic vulnerability but also elucidates the social consequences of being poor, illiterate, and dominated.

STUDY FINDINGS

This chapter draws on qualitative and ethnographic research data collected in the shanty towns in the city of Mohammedia near Casablanca. This chapter examines the way in which the mobile phone is used to create opportunities and social networks for female domestic workers. In addition to the ethnographic practice of participant observation, I conducted structured interviews using a questionnaire format with nineteen domestic workers or maids. Twelve of the nineteen maids are live-in domestic workers. The average age of the surveyed maids is twenty-eight years; they have lower levels of education when compared with the entire sample of this study: an average of 2 years of education contra 5.5 years for the whole surveyed sample ($n = 72$). Fifty-six percent have no formal schooling and are illiterate, 4.5 percent attended Quranic school, 39.5 percent attended primary school, and none attended secondary or postsecondary school or university.

Quantitative evidence on usage patterns of mobile phones for personal and business calls shows a monthly mean of forty-three personal calls and twenty-eight business calls per respondent. To measure the economic impact of the mobile phone on users' income and on shaping respondent social networks, I examined the pre- and post-mobile average incomes. For maids, the use of the mobile phone has led to an increase of 33 percent in their average monthly incomes, with *bricolage* or informal supplementary economic activity accounting for about 31 percent of their total income.

"SAINT MOBILE PHONE": MOBILE PHONE CHARISMA AND ECONOMIC EFFECTS

As my analysis suggests, there are a few contributing factors leading to this considerable increase in income. In addition to the regularity of *bricolage* jobs brought by the mobile phone, respondents acknowledged the economic contributions of the mobile phone to their livelihoods and emphasized its "help" in expanding their work opportunities. One maid, for instance, said,

> Before the mobile phone, we were deprived a lot. Now that I have a mobile phone, there is more revenue and there is more work. Occasional freelance or bricolage jobs in weddings, male circumcision events, and birthday and naming ceremonies, and other opportunities are available.

Wellman argues that with the rise of networked individualism, "mobile phones afford a fundamental liberation from place" in the sense that "their use shifts community ties from linking people-in-places to linking people wherever they are. Because the connection is the person, it shifts the dynamics of connectivity from places—typically households or worksites—to individuals" (2001, 238). As referenced in chapter 2, Donner (2006) reports that Rwandan micro-entrepreneurs use the mobile phone as a "job telephone" to increase the frequency of their contacts. Again, that seemed to hold true among the maids in this study. One maid said,

> *Al-portable*, even though I am illiterate, is good for finding work and avoiding old ways of searching for work. No need to go to the maid stand or do the tour of villas. Now, you leave your mobile number with maid friends, a store owner or a *samsar*. It is *'ajib* [amazing] for coordinating freelance and on-the-fly (*bricolat* and *ghafla*) jobs during weekends.

These accounts illustrate that the mobile phone appears to augment relationships with worker friends, middlemen, villa watchmen, or with families and neighbors. It provides an additional channel that seems to offer potential for economic productivity. Such intensification may ultimately depend on a *mélange* of networks from maid friends through *samsaras* to shopkeepers.

An effect of this simpler access to social networks is an augmented ability to engage in what the contacts of this study called *bricolage*, augmenting one's income by engaging in freelance labor. For the maids that were observed and interviewed, *bricolage* jobs include house cleaning, cooking, and preparing food for weddings, birthdays, naming ceremonies (*sbu'aa*) and male circumcision events, usually occurring after normal work hours or during weekends. My data also demonstrates that *bricolage* accounts for about 31 percent of a maid's monthly income. For the maids, the mobile also enabled them to serve multiple households, allowing them to be more fluid in their location and engagement of work.

The maid's modest face-to-face networks and acquaintances, now augmented with the mobile phone, represent the way that new technologies succeed by adding to existing systems and networks. The mobile provides the maid an instant connection into a network of trusted contacts. Rahma, for instance, said,

> *Al-portable* allows me to communicate with other maids for preparing difficult meals or desserts I am not used to making; to meet friends even briefly at the end of the street; and it is useful for employment seeking and *bricolage*. Buying a mobile phone is a worthy investment.

For Rahma, the mobile provides a chance to "link-up" with a potential freelance work opportunity (Horst and Miller 2005, 2006). The mobile also provides the opportunity to enhance her social ties—her presence within the network and stronger reciprocal bonds with those with whom she has been engaged. She now has a chance for much desired freelance work. The network of stores/*samsaras*/ neighbors/work friends/work site/villa guards, and the work carried on at these places, is made more valuable by the presence of the mobile phone. Another maid, Rabi'a, told me,

> *Al-portable* is the opportunity opener since work is never permanent. I leave my number with friends, neighbors, shopkeepers, *samsaras*, drug stores, and even at the bureau of labor. In *al-portable* there is *l'khir* [goodness] *and l'baraka*; it is like a *siyid* or patron-saint; it is a miracle-worker and those who invented *sidi al-portable* [saint mobile phone] should have shrines built for them so that we can do our *ziyaras* [ritualized visits] there. *Al-portable* brings me additional work, and that is a good thing when you are always short on money.

The Arabic word *l'baraka* or *baraka* means "blessedness," and in Morocco, it refers to a mysterious, miracle-working force, which is viewed as a blessing from God and may be simply translated in English by the words "divine blessings or holiness." Westermarck writes, "No man has possessed more *baraka* than the Prophet Muhammad. His *baraka* was transmitted to the shereefs (*shurfa*), that is the descendants in the male line of his daughter Fatimah" (1968, 36). In many cases, *baraka* is not limited to human beings but also attributed to nonhuman miracle-working entities and objects of worship such as water of springs, seawater, trees, stones, caves, rocks, animals, mountains, stars, and so on. In other words, *baraka* is almost everywhere and animates almost everything in Morocco (see also Geertz 1968; Gellner 1969; Eickelman 2002; Hammoudi 1997).

Moroccan Islam, or so-called popular Islam, is well-known for the ubiquity of "patron-saints" and their shrines, who are believed to work as helpful intermediaries in securing God's blessings for their disciples. Eickelman has described the role and place of patron-saints in Moroccan society as follows,

> Of course, the radio says that everything comes directly from God. But just as the king has his ministers, God has his [pious ones]. If you need a paper from the government office, which is better? Do you go straight to the official and ask for it? You might wait a long time and never receive it. Or do you go to someone who knows you and also knows the official? Of course, you go to the friend, who presents the case to the official. Same thing . . . if you want something from God. (Eickelman 2002, 274)

Charisma, Weber writes, "is a certain quality of an individual personality by virtue of which he is set apart from ordinary men and treated as endowed with supernatural, superhuman, or at least specifically exceptional powers or qualities" (1968b, 48). Weber describes forms of charismatic authority in which forces go into humans and animals, as well as objects (Weber 1968a). For Weber, charismatic authority is not just a quality of a person or an object, but also a magical, exceptional, or religious power endowed with the ability to stir up awe and stimulate change. In conditions where the force or *baraka* is believed to be within a thing or an object, this object becomes both powerful and a thing of vast value and reverence. It is within *depersonalized charisma* that charismatic, animated objects such as the mobile phone, for instance, influence human action and shape peoples' ways of envisioning the world and how it works (Weber 1968a, 1136).

Ames, for example, in her ethnographic account of the One Laptop per Child project, writes, "Charismatic technologies help establish and reinforce the ideological underpinnings of the status quo. They do so through promises that may persist among true believers even when the technology does not deliver" (2015, 111). However, Ames does not distinguish between assumptions and beliefs that motivate different technologies. While she provides a framework for making sense of the imagined transformations made by designers and technology promoters about their technological devices, this framework does not provide the means to account for how the mobile phone is perceived as a charismatic technology. Mobile phones, in my study, unlike the One Lap Per Child project analyzed by Ames (2019), are not conceptualized as status-quo safeguarding technologies but rather as convivial tools allowing "each person who uses them the greatest opportunity to enrich the environment with the fruits of his or her vision . . . [and] to express his meaning in action" (Illich 1973, 21–22).

Furthermore, seeing the mobile phone as a *charismatic subject*—as a saint/helper—with agency demonstrates key elements of Latour's ANT and Mauss' total social fact theory. In this view, charisma or *baraka* properties of the mobile phone, like "scripts" or programs of action built into technologies, are rooted in its compelling promise to act as an effective agent for better socioeconomic conditions. Additionally, one may argue that patron-saints of old are no longer firmly lodged in specific places and people, and the offerings and annual sacrifices, as well as "closeness" to a saint and his descendants, are slowly becoming rituals of the past. Following the maid Rabi'a's logic, each mobile phone is believed to exist and act as its own "digital patron-saint" on the go. In the recent past, Moroccans have called on patron-saints in particular places and times to act as their intermediaries with God and among people. In a parallel way, mobile phones are "filled' with *baraka* and thought to be negotiators between people and economic and social opportunities. With the convenience of portable pocket saints, so to speak, maids have been enabled to unlock and download *baraka* opportunity flows made accessible by the network effects of mobile telephony. As a result of this connectivity, there is no need for making time- and place-specific offerings and sacrifices, save for required payments of air-time top-ups, slight repairs, and availability of network coverage; and "just as the king has his ministers, God has his [pious ones]," maids have charismatic mobile phones with always-on miracle-working competencies to exploit information and energy *baraka* of networks, and in the process, to transform their social and economic lives at any time and from anywhere.

MOBILE PHONES, MEDIATED SOCIABILITY, AND SOCIAL CONTROL

Besides creating social networks, making money, and saving time, what other benefits do mobile phones bring to domestic workers? As indicated in their narratives, maids can face difficult situations; some find themselves in abusive and restrictive circumstances; and many face feelings of isolation and loneliness, especially live-in maids. Khadija, a live-in maid who hails from a nearby rural area, stressed the fact that parents of rural maids usually request that employers not let their daughters go out in public without supervision. She told me the story of a maid from a rural area who was asked by her employer to wash their new car but inadvertently washed the neighbor's car instead. She relayed this story to underscore the fact that this maid was kept inside the house to such an extent that she could not distinguish between her employer's car and that of the neighbor's.

All the maids report that the mobile phone enabled them to stay connected—with their parents, friends, and other maids, something they could not previously do. Several maids told me that the mobile phone has become an indispensable way of banishing the loneliness they feel while going about their daily chores and easing their suffocating social milieu. Khadija also reported,

> *Al-portable* is very important. I used to get news of family and friends once or twice a month. Now, I get news instantly and if only I could read, I would get even texting news and happenings. *Al-portable*, (*bash mazyan bazaf, kay ifaji al hmum, kay kharraj min al-diqah, ukay ifarah, ukay ihyi-rrahim*) is great in many aspects because it allows me to lighten my burdens, to release my pressures and stress, to brighten or make one's day happy, and to refresh one's ties of kinship. Now, I can call my parents and can call upon my other maid friends in case of emergency, disputes, or any need.

The deployment of the mobile phone in sustaining and nurturing traditional social obligations is not unique to Moroccan mobile phone users. Foster and Horst (2018), for instance, examine how people living across the Pacific Islands use mobile phones to strengthen and expand social relationships and intimacy within the context of moral economy. Among the people of Sepik River of Papua New Guinea, Lipset (2018) shows that people use mobile phones to maintain and strengthen kinship ties across physical distances. Similarly, Wardlow (2018) frames the mobile phone as an "affective technology," as it was used by the women of Tari, Papua New Guinea, to create and foster emotional intimacy and spiritual support with their kin and make "phone friends," who could be perceived as intimate strangers known only through mobile phones. Through mobile phones, women, especially HIV-positive women experiencing social isolation and stigma, were empowered to form connections with their phone friends and thus obtain emotional and spiritual support.

Mobile telephony has enabled maids to communicate more easily and more effectively with friends, neighbors, families, and coworkers. Social obligations and bonds no longer involve face-to-face-interactions, and almost every aspect of a maid's life has been mediated with the mobile phone. Kriem observed that in Morocco, "the use of telephony in the maintenance of *silatu rahim* [bonds of kinship] is significant in light of the extraordinary importance this social practice enjoys in Islam" (2009, 206). Provided that maids, in general, inhabit a circumscribed physical and emotional space, the mobile phone has come to represent both an opening through which daily pressure and stress are channeled and released and a way to extend their communicative reach to family and friend networks.

The respondents also discussed some undeniable disadvantages of mobile phone access and use in terms of power and gender relationships. One maid, Malika, when asked about the social implications of mobile phone use, said,

There is a negative aspect to the mobile for a woman who carries it because people think she has gone astray and has no good morals (*kharja al-tariq, mam-zyanash*). It can become a problem. People think you are loose and can circulate . . . my fiancé wanted to change my number and only wants the number for himself. Nowadays, individual and complete freedom or doing what you think you want to do appears to exist only before engagement or marriage. During marriage preparations, the first thing that must go is the SIM card and a new SIM card must be obtained, and your fiancé or potential husband wants the new number only for himself.

What is striking in the aforementioned quote is the explicit reference to the loss of freedom or sense of being in control for a woman who owns a mobile phone but who is pondering the idea of getting involved in either a romantic adventure or a potential marriage lead. Several maids see the mobile phone as a means of control and surveillance used by men to control their communicative reach and movement; this sentiment is clearly articulated in the aforementioned example in which a maid is made to change her subscriber identity module (SIM) card or mobile phone once engaged or married. What is remarkable here too is the parallels that the maid draws between the SIM card and freedom and trust before and after marriage. The SIM card before engagement or marriage appears to be the part of the mobile phone that allows her to be free; where her places, people, and secrets reside.

In Arabic, the linguistic roots of the words *hurriyah* (freedom) and *hurr* (free) do not stand for democratic values as understood in Western democratic societies. Mernissi explains,

On the contrary, *hurr* is what distinguishes a person from being a slave, from being inferior. . . . [It] is associated with aristocratic sovereignty and not with the struggle against despotism. . . . [It] is a concept intrinsically linked to *sharaf* [honor], the aristocracy, the elite, the superior group" (Mernissi 1997, 15).

Equally significant in this context are cultural norms of sexuality and gender roles, and how men and women differ as persons. Rosen, for instance, reported that Moroccans distinguish three essential properties of human nature: *ruh* (soul), *nafs* (passions and desires), and *'aqel* (reason and rationality). *Ruh* refers to a person's soul; soul comes from God and it will return to Him after one's death. *Nafs* is in all living creatures, including men, angels, animals, and the invisible spirits or creatures (*jnun*). *Nafs* is made of passions and lusts, and if it is not brought under control, it creates disorder and shameful behavior. *'Aqel* is "reason, rationality, the ability to use our heads in order to keep our passions from getting hold of us and controlling us. God gave Adam reason so he would know good from bad" (1984, 31). Through education and following the teachings of Islam, man can cultivate rational capabilities to keep himself from being a slave to his passions. Women also have reason but are not able to nurture it as fully as men. Rosen (1984) writes,

> It is just in their nature. Women have very great sexual desires and that is why a man is always necessary to control them, to keep them from creating all sorts of disorder. . . . Why else do we call women *hbal shaitan*, "the rope of Satan." That is why women must be cloaked when in public, live in houses with small windows placed so others cannot see in, and married off before they can give their fathers any trouble. It's like the saying goes: "A woman by herself is like a Turkish bath without water." Because she is always hot and without a man, she has no way to slake the fire. (1984, 32–33)

Indeed, the mobile phone has revealed itself as a central authority on the ways men and women negotiate issues around trust and gender ideologies. Archambault (2011), in her ethnography of mobile phones and intimate relationships in Mozambique, claims that mobile phone use often leads couples to break up. She also argues that mobile phones enable the free flow of information that is expected to remain secret, which ignites conflicts and misunderstandings between couples. Similarly, in Malika's experience, the mobile phone reveals the morally charged concepts of freedom, trust, and good and bad behavior, which are at stake in her decision to pursue a romantic or marriage relationship. In this sense, the removal of Malika's SIM card involves not only the remaking of the maid's identity and historical record (contacts, places, and secrets) but also the loss of her privacy, autonomy, and resistance to male domination and authority. Just as the Moroccan expression *'andha sharaf*, meaning "she has honor/she is a virgin," underscores the salient bond between female honor/virginity and marriage, it also comes with the cultural prerequisite that women in pursuit of marriage relations must also have "virgin" SIM cards, so to speak. At best, they must acquire new phones with new phone numbers, numbers that must be vetted by potential husbands before they are shared with other people. In sum, while the mobile is a saint that nurtures personal networking and economic opportunity, it also comes with the inherent feature of easier surveillance and other forms of control. These two latter features seem to clearly favor men who dominate women socially and disfavor those who occupy a position of subordination in society, as in the case of maids. Evidently, the mobile has not entirely revolutionized gender and patriarchy relations in Moroccan society.

CONCLUSION

In this chapter, I have demonstrated the economic and social relevance of the mobile phone as a tool of productivity and sociability to female domestic workers. The mobile phone practices discussed in this chapter speak to the social shaping of the mobile phone by maids who have adopted and incorporated this technology into their daily social and economic lives. Among the maids, the use of the mobile phone has allowed them to diversify the way in which they find employment opportunities and has resulted in increased income. It has also dispelled their loneliness and isolation, and it has become a channel for the release of daily pressures by allowing them to remain in contact with family, friends, and other social networks. In addition, for some maids, the mobile phone is a charismatic device, or a miracle-working saint, representing *baraka* (divine blessings) and enabling them to make connections and find work. In terms of power and gender relations in a society steeped in the dominant ideology of patriarchy, and despite the benefits offered to maids by the mobile phone, most maids view the mobile phone as a means of control by men over women.

Chapter 4

Smallholder Farmers

The Mobile Phone Is neither a Snowmobile nor a Truck

Agricultural decisions regarding timely soil preparation and planting, irrigation and weeding, cultivating and harvesting, and storage and marketing have always been key concerns to farmers. Although many forms of indigenous knowledge are still central in managing agriculture, ICTs have made an impact over the years. The introduction of mobile phones has been one of the most transformative of these ICTs in farming. They have sped up the ways in which farmers get, exchange, and manipulate information. They allow farmers to rework the way they interact with rural and urban markets. Increasingly, they enable farmers to focus, search, and extract useful and up-to-date market information from social and business networks. Farmers, who are now always accessible due to the mobile phone, are less constrained by time and place, and, as such, they can more easily make tentative decisions and take more risks.

In this chapter, I examine how mobile phones are used, and to what effect, by smallholder farmers in southern Morocco; I claim that mobile phones have deepened market participation by farmers, resulting in intensive cultivation of cash crops; and I contend that mobile telephony is a tool of reorganizing production and marketing strategies, leading to higher farming revenues. This chapter consists of five sections. The first section provides a theoretical framework of the mobile phone in the farming sector. The second provides a background on Moroccan agriculture and describes my research findings. The third deals with the mobile phone and the spirit of risk taking. The fourth delves into the use of the mobile phone for information search and the leveling of information asymmetry between farmers and middlemen. Finally, the last section discusses the ways in which mobile phones are different from old technologies such as snowmobiles and trucks.

THEORIZING THE MOBILE PHONE
IN THE FARMING SECTOR

There is growing literature on the impact of mobile phone use on agricultural activities and practices in the developing world. Mobile phones facilitate the dissemination of agricultural information to farming communities, enable farmers to carry out checks on market prices, and accelerate agricultural growth by facilitating knowledge management and planning. The rapid increase in the use of mobile phones worldwide has greatly influenced farming activities in various ways. The mobile phone has allowed for an increase in farmers' incomes, reduced information and transportation costs, made agricultural marketing more efficient, and empowered farmers to renegotiate their bargaining power and position within traditional trade relationships. Significantly, it has empowered farmers to engage directly with wholesalers, switch markets in response to better prices, and penetrate larger and more distant markets (Ilahiane 2007; World Bank 2013, 2016).

In Niger, Aker (2008, 2011) found that the expansion of mobile networks has positive effects on both traders and consumer welfare by decreasing grain price differences by 20 percent; reducing traders' search costs by 50 percent; increasing traders' profits by 29 percent; and reducing average consumer grain prices by 3.5 percent, which is equivalent to five to ten days of grain consumption annually. These results are not because more products were traded but because better prices were obtained through real-time market research made available by mobile phones. Moreover, Aker also reported that the use of mobile phones enabled traders to reach more markets and establish wider contacts. In Uganda, Muto et al. (2009) found that mobile phone coverage and information availability improved banana farming expansion, leading to greater market participation and a 10 percent rise in profits. In the Philippines, Labonne, and Chase (2009) reported that ownership of a mobile phone has a correlation with higher incomes, in the range of 11–17 percent, as measured through consumption behavior, as well as improved relationships with trading partners. In India, as mobile networks were expanding in coastal areas, Jensen (2007) found that fishermen who were previously ill-informed of daily prices in different markets were now able to contact various ports to find the best price for their catch. This resulted in more profit for fishermen as this information allowed them to sell their fish at the market where they obtained higher prices. Waste decreased and prices equalized throughout the regional port, and there were even small gains in consumer welfare. Röller and Waverman (2001) claimed that a developing country with an average of 10 or more mobile phones per 100 people would have enjoyed per capita GDP growth of 0.59 percent higher than an otherwise identical country with a mobile phone density of less than ten phones per 100 people.

The aforementioned studies discuss the benefits of the use of the mobile phone in the agriculture sector. However, there are cases where the mobile phone has shown little to no impact on the relationship between farmers and traders/middlemen. Molony (2008) conducted a study on the effects of mobile phones on traders/middlemen of perishable foodstuffs in Tanzania. In his study, due to the importance of credit in the relationship between farmers and these wholesale buyers, Molony found that the introduction of the mobile phone had no impact on these relationships, and therefore, farmers did not benefit as is found in other studies. Molony claims that farmers accepted the middlemen's prices for their crops because the middlemen also served as their creditors. Farmers were unable to leverage mobile phone-based information on market prices and potential buyers in other markets or areas as doing so would run the risk of damaging their relationship with a middleman who is also a supplier of much-needed credit and other services.

BACKGROUND ON MOROCCAN AGRICULTURE AND STUDY FINDINGS

Morocco, with a population of nearly 35 million people, is located on northwest coast of the African continent. Its arid to semi-arid physical geography consists of a wide variety of features ranging from mountains and plateaux, to inland and coastal plains, to oases and Saharan landscapes. Because of its arid environment, the country experiences diverse climatic conditions with large annual variability of precipitation. Morocco faces irregular rain patterns, along with cold spells and heat waves, increasingly resulting in droughts and dust storms, which significantly distress agricultural production.

In spite of these environmental constraints, farming remains the main driver for the Moroccan economy, contributing 14 to 20 percent of the country's GDP, and representing 43 percent of all employment and 78 percent of rural employment. Eighty percent of arable lands are located in arid or semi-arid areas and only 15 percent of the country's agricultural land is irrigated. The average farm size is 5.7 hectares. The agricultural sector consists of both large-scale commercial farms and small-scale farms. Large-scale agricultural operations are concentrated in irrigated areas and, although representing only 15 percent of agricultural lands, contribute about 45 percent to the national GDP and represent 75 percent of agricultural exports. They export large portions of cash crops such as citrus fruits and a wide range of vegetables and legumes. Smallholder or subsistence farming is found in rain-fed areas and produces mainly cereal, livestock, olives, dates, vegetables, and fruit. Smallholder farming contributes to the GDP by growing mainly food crops and selling locally for lower profit. This lower profit is attributed to the difficulties small-scale farmers experience in finding successful and profitable paths to markets. Additionally, the rural population that represents nearly 44 percent of the Moroccan population is mostly composed of smallholder farmers whose production depends almost entirely on rainfall. The gross annual agricultural product is strongly correlated with the annual rainfall, and, due to the economic significance of the agricultural sector, each rainfall deficit impacts the entire economy of the country (Ghanem 2015).

The Plan Maroc Vert or PMV (Green Morocco Plan), which was launched in 2008 and ran until 2020, sought to modernize Moroccan agriculture and to develop the country's rural areas by focusing on large farms, mostly export oriented. As the national agricultural policy of the country, the plan identified two major objectives: (1) to double agricultural GDP and (2) to double agricultural income in order to reduce poverty. With an investment of more than US$10 billion, the PMV supported both irrigation and mechanization, along with the processing of agricultural products and the use of genetically improved seeds. The plan also included the construction of dams, the expansion of irrigation, and the conversion of crops to those better suited to local climates. One component involved planting fruit and olive trees in former grain producing areas. While many of the plan's objectives were seen as beneficial, some critics believe it gave priority to large commercial and industrial farming. There is a concern that the government, urged along by international development organizations and commercial seed and chemical corporations, is pushing forward a model of intensive agriculture that is dependent on the global market and free trade. Others argue that increasing food reserves, improving links to markets, and supporting the development of independent producer organizations should be the priority of government policy. This would strengthen the resilience of smallholders and enable them to contribute meaningfully to sustainable food production for Morocco (Ghanem 2015).

This chapter draws on ethnographic research on mobile phone use and economic productivity among smallholder farmers in the Ziz River Valley of the Errachidia region. As discussed in the introduction of this book, the Ziz River Valley's smallholder agriculture is concentrated mainly in intensive irrigated farming of cereals, alfalfa, vegetables, dates, olives, apples, peaches, and livestock raising. I examined the way in which the mobile phone is put to economic use to create and augment business opportunities and social networks. In addition to the ethnographic practice of participant observation, I conducted structured interviews using a questionnaire format with twenty-one male farmers. The average age of my respondents is 40.08 years. Most have been schooled in Quranic school or in public educational institutions: 8.3 percent attended Quranic school, 33.3 percent attended primary school, 33.3 percent attended secondary school, and 25 percent attended university. The average number of years of education is 9.3. In terms of household conjugal status and size, 91.7 percent were married, 8.3 percent were single, with an average of 5.3 persons per household. As for the ethnic composition of the sample, 33 percent were Arab, 37 percent were Amazigh (Berber), and 30 percent Haratine (blacks).

To gain a broad understanding of the context of mobile phones in the lives of farmers, I collected information on the presence of traditional modes and means of social contact and media use. With respect to ownership of traditional technologies of communication and mobility, the mean number of bicycles per farmer surveyed was 2.5, mopeds stood at 1.5, video players stood at 0.25, radios at 2.17, television sets at 2.25, and satellite dishes at 1.6. For comparison, the average number of mobile phones per farmer surveyed is 2.33 and the number of mobile phones acquired over the last five years is 2.82. While none owns a personal computer and access to the internet is insignificant, all farmers had mobile phones, and four had a complementary landline at home; internet access was limited to the use of cybercafes.

Quantitative evidence on usage patterns of mobile phones for personal and business calls shows a monthly mean of 44.5 personal calls and 157.7 business calls per respondent. The analysis also shows that respondents spend a monthly average of 200 Moroccan dirhams (US$20) on prepaid calling cards for their mobile phones, and about 120 Moroccan dirhams (US$12) on public pay phones. To assess the economic impact of the mobile phone on farmers' incomes and on shaping respondent social networks, I examined the pre- and post-mobile average incomes. The analysis indicates that mobile phone use has resulted in an increase of 23.7 percent in farmers' annual incomes. Further emphasizing that access to mobile phones creates economic opportunities, I also found that, in my sample, one additional mobile phone creates about six permanent jobs, results in a percentage of change in labor recruitment of 93.45, and travels an average distance of 453.75 kilometers (281.94 miles).

In Morocco, agricultural produce is sold in a variety of ways and places. Depending on the location, personal ability and connections, and the quantity of harvest, farmers have several options for the sale of their produce. Urban and rural towns have *suqs* or markets where merchants sell a variety of products and each *suq* has a section that specifically sells agricultural products. Farmers who sell their produce in *suqs* often cannot get into the cities to sell directly. As a result, farmers have depended on ambulant merchants and peddlers, called *sbaybiyah* in colloquial Moroccan Arabic, who travel from place to place to buy produce from farmers and resell it at a higher price at significant profit. For these ambulant merchants, being a *sbaybee* is a full- or part-time occupation, albeit unregulated. These itinerant merchants are arbitrageurs "who gain their living out of the differential between what something sells for in one marketplace and what it sells for in another to which they can readily transport it" (Geertz 1979, 188).

Before the mobile phone, farmers mainly sold their produce to itinerant peddlers and other small-scale intermediaries, putting farmers at a disadvantage and making it harder for them to earn a substantial profit from their produce. Since most farmers did not have access to market information nor the means to travel to markets themselves, most were unaware of their crops' real-time market prices and profitability. With the uptake of the mobile phone, farmers increasingly spoke and engaged directly with wholesalers or larger-scale intermediaries. Thirty percent of the survey sample made the shift from dealing with small itinerant peddlers to dealing directly with wholesalers in major cities (cf. Molony 2008). Farmers also coordinated with local truckers to improve product transportation, allowing them to switch markets to capture better prices. A farmer told me that he once was on his way to sell some of his livestock and produce in one market, but in the middle of the journey, he received a call from a contact in another market who told him that there were better prices there, and (tout de suite or right on the spot) he made a U-turn and headed to the market that had better prices for livestock and produces. Most respondents increasingly speak of their wholesale clients, and less of the traditional links to itinerant intermediaries or *sbaybiyah*, and how the mobile phone has extended the radius of distance their produce travels; it travels in all directions (see figure 4.1).

Respondents also recognized the economic contributions of the mobile to the bottom line of their farming operations and emphasized its "help" in expanding the scope and scale of their marketing options. One farmer, for instance, said that

> now I have clients for my carrots in the north of Morocco, about 600 kilometers (372.82 miles) from Errachidia. I am no longer 100 percent tied to (dishonest) intermediaries, or to the dusty, sleepy, markets in our area. My carrots are in demand in the north and the mobile has made their travel there easy and economical to maintain.

This little bit of connectivity seems to be making a major difference in farming and marketing decisions, as well as optimizing farmers' time and operations.

Another important change was that farmers used their new knowledge to become more market oriented in their production, moved away from producing low-value crops, and diversified into higher-value enterprises. Of the survey sample, 40 percent of respondents planned to cultivate cash crops (mostly vegetables and fruits); 20 percent planned to increase the acreage devoted to alfalfa as it constitutes the main feed for livestock (sheep and cattle); and 35 percent planned to plant olives, dates, apples, almonds, walnuts, and other market friendly trees. The knowledge gained from using the mobile phone

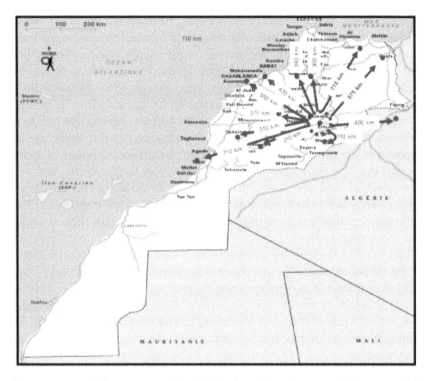

Figure 4.1   Marketing Patterns of Agricultural Produce from Errachidia. Created by author, drawing on map available at routard.com.

enabled farmers to take risks (*za'aama*) on crop planting and marketing. As one carrot farmer put it: "*al-portable kay eza'aam*": the mobile phone stimulates risk taking, or *za'aama*, when it comes to planning crop planting and response to market signals and needs.

THE MOBILE PHONE AND THE
SPIRIT OF RISK TAKING

A relevant finding was that mobile phones changed farmers' behavior related to risk taking. The easier access to market information via the mobile phone provided the farmers with an enhanced ability to engage in what they called *za'aama* (risk-taking leadership or pioneership) and *al-tawakkul 'ala Allah* (reliance on God). Hence, the farmers now felt they had the capacity to rely on God and to take risks by responding to market needs and signals. In Arabic, the terms *za'aama* or *za'im* (leader, head, boss, or strong man) culturally refer to charismatic and authoritarian political leadership in the Middle

East and North Africa. In its classic meaning, *za'aama* is a political term and it refers to a type of Arab political leadership in which a recognized leader has the power to speak for the interests of his clients, and to whom clients will go if they have business and other affairs to negotiate with stronger partners than themselves (see Hottinger 1961; Sharabi 1963; Moaddel 2002). The appropriation of the term *za'aama/za'im* by farmers from its political context is quite striking. From the Moroccan farmers' perspective, the terms *za'aama* and *za'im* stand for taking risks and leading the way in the use and adoption of the mobile phone in farming. In mobilizing the power of mobile phones, they see themselves as paving a new way to do farming and view themselves as bold and as trailblazing as a *za'im* would be during times of change. They are *za'ims*, not in the political sense of the term, but in their willingness to take a risk on this new technology to change their economic and social relationships.

Farmers also spoke of the concept of *al-tawakkul 'ala Allah* in the context of risk taking. *Al-tawakkul 'ala Allah* is a concept in Islamic theology, especially that of Sufis or mystics, meaning reliance upon God. In Islam, there is a debate about the virtues of "earning a living" (*kasb*) versus putting one's pure trust in God's plan to the point of fatalism and laziness (Lewisohn 2020). The central issue in this debate is whether *tawakkul* allows for the use of intermediary causes provided by God to make a living and shape one's livelihood or if *tawakkul* only allows for a more passive approach to earning one's living. Farmers shared with me the Moroccan saying in which Allah exhorts people to implement His intermediary causes: *tsabbab ya 'abdi, wana n-kamalik* (oh my slave, implement the intermediary causes, or means, I have put at your disposition and I will help you complete your goals). In this instance, the intermediary causes—after putting one's trust in God—are mobile phones and they are deployed to expand and create market opportunities. In Islam, practicing *tawakkul* produces determination, strength, and an acceptance of God's will and plan. It also keeps worry and disappointment at a minimum and gives farmers energy and hope to take risks and to take account of themselves and their future actions to lead a pious and prosperous life. For farmers, *tawakkul* and hard work are a form of worship (*'ibada*).

Consider the telling situation of Youssef. Youssef owns seven hectares of land and grows a variety of fruit trees and crops: dates, figs, olives, almonds, peaches, wheat, barley, alfalfa, carrots, beets, onions, mint, and a variety of herbs. He also raises two cows and has thirty head of sheep. For Youssef, the mobile is ideal for making calls, getting price information, and negotiating prices. It is good for recruiting laborers and for getting market and family news. He said that "al-portable *kay enddam al-khadma,* it organizes work. It increases the impulse of *z'aama* and *tawakkul*, provides peace of mind (*raht al-baal*), and helps with recruiting and checking upon laborers (*al-khaddama*)." The power of the mobile resides in its *awal* or talk ability as "we don't have time for writing. It is talk, talk, and talk; I can call the regional veterinarian at any time when my livestock is feeling sick. It has helped me with decision-making." Now, because of access to real-time market information, Youssef plans to expand the area devoted to alfalfa from 0.25 hectare to 1 hectare and carrots, beets, and onions to 0.5 hectare each. He also plans to increase the number of sheep from 30 to 80 head and cattle from two to four head.

Consider, as another example, the view of Hammoo on the implications of the mobile phone to his farming operations. Hammoo owns 12 hectares of land and grows apples, peaches prunes, pomegranates, pears, grapes, alfalfa, wheat, green beans, maize, potatoes, carrots, almonds, and walnuts. For Hammoo, the mobile is the best way to get to know people, meaning buyers and sellers, and it allows farmers to act on market information, or "the news of the market." Hammoo said that

> one mobile phone equals the work of 10 people in the chain of production and having and using a mobile is having peace of mind. Middlemen or *sbaybiyah* are thieves and a source of incessant *al-waswas* (anxiety). With the availability of produce storage facilities and market information brought by the mobile, I no longer sell produce on trees (stand sale). I only sell produce on trees when it is a bad production.

Equally significant, Hammoo adds, "the mobile is '*ftuh arrahba*,'" which literally means "the opening of the grain market." In Moroccan Sufi rituals, the concept *ftuh arrahba* refers to the opening song and dance portion of an-all night possession ceremony, also called *lila* or *derdba*. This opening ritual sets the stage for summoning several spirit masters (*mluk*). These spirit masters are called upon for their protection and their power to cure all sorts of social, economic, and psychological conditions. Outside of Sufi possession séances, *ftuh arrahba* takes the form of a fee, or *dirham l'ftuh*, paid to traditional religious healers (i.e., *fqih*) for their curing services. The fee, Westermarck writes, "is as necessary for the recovery of the patient as is a key for the opening of a lock" (1968, 156). For Hammoo, the mobile phone represents a powerful communication assistant or master key/spirit in unlocking and opening the gate of opportunities. The mobile is not only unlocking and summoning information from distant marketplaces—places that are full of thievery, deception, and fraud—but also serving as a shield of protection to Hammoo from unreliable marketplace information. It ensures reliable payments and allows him to represent himself in his business transactions which has helped him recover from predatory trading relationships. Indeed, Hammoo has no love for middlemen and said,

I must tell you also that I lost lots of money over the years because I trusted middlemen I did not know. I took their checks for goods that turned out to be empty and bad. Now, I no longer use their services and I have become my own representative to wholesalers and to larger intermediaries in major cities. You can say that I am a farmer and a trader at the same time now.

Likewise, for Moha, the use of the mobile means that time is saved, less money is spent on transportation, and more information about the *inghmisen n-suq* (market information) is gathered in real-time. He adds,

With the mobile phone, your payment is guaranteed (*tadmant rzaq nnak*); the never-ending problem of the middlemen (*ikkas lmashakil n'sbaybiya*) is removed. Because of dishonesty (*qallat al-ma'qul* or *ikhudaan*) and fraudulent practices of middlemen, I was the victim of three bad checks from different greedy middlemen before the advent of the mobile phone. Now with the mobile, my payment is guaranteed because the mobile number of the buyer is trackable, and I also do not have to sell my produce to middlemen. Also, a loss of 10 percent to dishonest buyers is still better than empty or bad checks.

Farmers reported that the mobile phone enabled them to renegotiate the terms of information asymmetry and unequal trade relationships between sellers and buyers, something they could not previously do. Additionally, for many in my study, the mobile incentivized them to take the path of *al-tawakkul* to expand their farming operations by enabling them to become risk-takers, leaders and pioneers, allowing them to be more active in farming decision-making processes and engagement of trading relationships. The mobile allowed them to act as both a farmer and as their own agent in business relationships. It allowed them to level the playing field of information asymmetry, and empowered them to remove deceptive payment practices they suffered over the decades, thereby, they were empowered to develop new farming strategies, add value to their crops, and raise their farming incomes.

INFORMATION SEARCH AND THE FLATTENING OF INFORMATION ASYMMETRY

When asked about reasons for the purchase of a mobile phone, one farmer responded,

That is an easy question! Before *al-portable*, there was a lot of waste. After *al-portable*, *aqqarrab al-masafa*, it made the distant nearby. It helps me decide what to do with my produce. It is all profits. When it is time to sell olives, you know the price of olives and you have the choice to either sell your produce on trees (stand sale) or turn it into oil, or both. It is all wins: time saved; easy transport arrangement; no thieves; no risks; I can send money via post and avoid all sorts of harm.

Another farmer added that

seasonal production such as vegetables and fruits go in parallel with the mobile phone market information versus annual crops. It helps me know the needs of the market and gives me flexibility of decision making to respond to short-term needs of consumers. With the mobile, and if you have the means, you stay in place to do things. I use the mobile to track the trips of my produce since I use several transportation modes to ship it, from public buses to informal means of transport to shared rentals of trucks. When I travel to far away markets such as Berkane (600 kilometers (373 miles)) to sell my vegetables or fruit, I make sure that I bring back oranges to sell back home. I cannot afford to drive an empty truck back home. You see, if you are clever enough, and as the popular saying goes "*ki-al manchaar, tala' wakel, habit wakel*: like a saw with its sharp blade cutting through when going up and cutting through when going down," you can play the roles of the middleman and farmer in selling and buying deals at the same time.

Undeniably, farmers have exploited and pioneered the coordination and organization capabilities of mobile phone. They obtain real-time market pricing information via mobile phones, saving time and travel, making them better-informed about where and at what price to sell their products, thereby raising their incomes and improving the sustainability of their livelihoods. Farmers value mobile phones as fast and convenient ways to communicate with various stakeholders in the agricultural value chain and to get prompt answers with respect to problems they face in growing crops and raising livestock. The mobile phone also creates opportunities relative to getting marketing and weather information. Through mobile phones, farmers can directly keep in touch with many clients in various marketplaces and offer their produce at competitive prices.

The use of the mobile phone also empowers farmers to be aware of real-time weather forecasts. As one farmer put it,

Apple farming in the desert is hard and it is like the United States fighting in Iraq! We are suffering, we are stuck, and we are left with no help or assistance from the government. If I grew alfalfa or cereals, I would leave farming right now, but apples trees are an investment, and I cannot leave them behind. Gas charges for pumping water costs 200 dirhams per week (about US$20). Add to that recurrent river floods, flash floods, scirocco winds, and sandstorms. And God save us, *tamorghi* or locust threats. And if that is not enough, I am indebted to *boo idiwan* (pesticide seller), *boo langri* (fertilizer seller) and *boo l-credit* (bank loan officer). When prices are low and our local markets are too full of the same things that we grow, and if I can afford it, I store some of my agricultural produce in a storage facility for about 5 months. Weather forecasting information available in the portable is a great thing in the punitive environment of the desert. Do not forget to jot down that frost and snow damage farming here. We can lose 50 percent of our crops when we are not aware of the weather conditions as in the case of the scirocco winds and frost.

Four decades ago, Geertz (1979) discussed the nature and functioning of the Moroccan suq or the "bazaar-type economy" in which markets coexisted with a mixture of old and new institutions and rituals. For Geertz, the central question was the absence in the suq of firm-type organization, with all the market information and institutions that it entails in the West: product standardization, advertising, and brand names. In the Sefrou suq, Geertz argues that a lack of reliable information in the marketplace meant that

> information is generally poor, scarce, maldistributed, inefficiently communicated, and intensely valued. . . . The level of ignorance about everything from product quality and going prices to market possibilities and production costs is very high. . . . The search for information one lacks and the protection of information one has is the name of the game. (1979, 124–125)

Trade in the bazaar was organized around the attempt to control the flow of information: to find out (or hide) the going price for a given good or to identify (or hide) the qualities of goods subject to exchange. Because success in the bazaar was dependent on controlling information, this fact makes it much harder for all participants to grow and prosper. In the suq, according to Geertz, the lack of reliable market information was channeled through a good deal of bargaining along with intensive information search regarding the price and quality of goods. From an information and communication view, Geertz writes,

> The most important is that search more readily takes the form of exploring matters in depth with particular partners rather than surveying widely through the market, a case approach rather than a sampling one, or what Rees called an intensive as opposed to an extensive strategy (1979, 223–224).

He says that a successful modernization of the bazaar economy would require "increasing its capacity to inform its participants" (1979, 234).

Among farmers using mobile phones, Geertz's insights regarding *suq* bargaining and information search practices seem not to remain entirely true, as illustrated in many stories from my contacts. Information asymmetry in the past has made farmers vulnerable to middlemen and has hampered their access to key information on framing, transportation, and marketing. Every one of my respondents had a story about how the mobile phone is not just a means of knowing what is happening in local and nonlocal markets but also a major driver behind their decisions to alter the terms of bargaining and flatten information asymmetry in the marketplace. In fact, the mobile phone appears to blur the distinction between intensive/clientalized and extensive modalities of information search. As a communication channel used for gathering information on prices of goods and manipulation of variations in different marketplaces by the now always-accessible farmer, the mobile phone succeeds in affecting bargaining and the balance of power in the farmer to middleman relationship. Viewed through this lens, the mobile phone has allowed farmers to shift their economic behavior from a mode of intensive search, establishing enduring trade relationships with specific buyers, to a mode of extensive search, in which farmers canvass widely and make decisions based on known prices of produce in different markets and areas. With the use of the mobile phone, farmers are empowered to engage in extensive searches for high-intensity partners without competing for the same partner; and in leveraging extensive searches, clientalization and market bargaining are no longer as important as they used to be in the pre-mobile phone era. As the traditional market information situation shifts in favor of farmers, they are likely to force middlemen into competition with each other because farmers are now engaged in extensive searches rather than intensive ones. Thereby, farmers are well positioned not only to extract favorable prices from different partners in different marketplaces for their produce, but in some cases, they may cut out the middlemen from the chain of produce marketing (cf. Geertz 1979; see also Napora 2011; Greenberg and Park 2017).

THE MOBILE PHONE IS NEITHER A
SNOWMOBILE NOR A TRUCK

The preceding sections explore the advantages of mobile phone ownership. All the surveyed respondents stressed the importance of owning a mobile phone, and they also emphasized the fact that by the mere fact of having one, one has access to market information and can renegotiate the terms of marketing information and create opportunities. One might still ask the question: How does the mobile phone compare as an investment to other modernization options?

Although the mobile phone shares several mobility properties such as coordination and speeding up of economic activities with other traditional types of technology, mobile phone technology is different in many ways and for various reasons. Chatty (1996), for instance, in her ethnography on mobile pastoralists, argues that the introduction of the truck among the Bedouin pastoralists of Oman coupled with the establishment of infrastructure in the 1970s had far-reaching consequences. Trucks replaced camels and were used to transport flocks from the desert to distant marketplaces; to transport households and flocks from one camp to another; and to bring water to the herds instead of driving the herds of goats and camels to the water. Trucks also provided easy connections between villages and nomadic encampments, allowing some pastoralists to engage in a variety of seasonal migration, partial sedentism, and wage labor.

The speed with which the truck replaced the camel, Chatty argues, altered pastoralists' concept of time and distance, deskilled their knowledge and survival skills, redefined their migrations and settlement patterns, and led to major threats to the long-term sustainability of pastoralism. She writes,

> In the past range usufruct depended on two factors. First, up to two or three weeks were required to move from one pasture to another. Today that can take a matter of hours or days by truck. This rapid mobility, in the past two decades, led to increased overgrazing of the rangeland. Second, there was the almost universal seizure of tribal territory by the nation-state and its transformation into a state-owned land. This has removed the tribal leaders from the protective and regulative role they once fulfilled in the pastoral community. (1996, 22)

In the same vein, Pelto (1973) argues that the replacement of dog sleds and reindeer sleds by the snowmobile in the 1960s had sweeping consequences in the Arctic region. He argues that snowmobiles quickly replaced reindeer sleds and had the advantage of fast travel. Pelto and Muller-Wille write,

> Compared to the slowness of dog sled and reindeer travel, the snowmobile presented the people of the Arctic with truly astonishing new mobility. In northeastern Finnish Lapland the market trips to Norway that once required three days can now be completed in six hours. What had been a two-day journey from the Tsiuttijoki roundup site to Sevettijarvi village is now an easy four hours. (1972, 189–190)

Pelto (1973) adds that the snowmobile, with its constant need for maintenance and fuel, forced the integration of the indigenous reindeer pastoralists of the Arctic into a global and monetized economy. This created, he claims, new dependencies in former subsistence communities, a process he calls delocalization, especially on gasoline consumption and repairs, wage labor, and debt from nonlocal resources. Pelto and Muller-Wille (1972) also contend that this transition from local economic autonomy to economic interdependence with the outside society led to increased social stratification and involved "the increased decimation of game, noise pollution of the backlands, junkyard effects of retired machines, air pollution from combustion engines, and many other effects" (Pelto and Muller-Wille 1972, 197), and may have hastened the end of traditional nomadism among reindeer herders in the Arctic region.

When comparing mobile phones to snowmobiles and trucks, it is noteworthy to observe the differences in the trends associated with the economic advantages of each of these technologies. While the costs of owning a truck or a snowmobile, or other forms of transportation can be seen to have continuously risen, the direct costs of mobile phone ownership in Morocco have decreased considerably, the result of the opening up of the Moroccan telecommunications markets discussed earlier, the appearance of prepaid usage options, user cost-reduction techniques (i.e., beeping), and the generally declining cost per capability ratio associated with electronic goods as exemplified in what has come to be known as "Moore's Law."

Figures 4.2 and 4.3 summarize the primary economic advantages of snowmobile and mobile phone ownership. With respect to snowmobiles, the figure shows that the direct costs of snowmobile ownership have increased, while there has been a decrease in the relative economic advantage of ownership. Mobile phones appear to create the opposite economic effects of

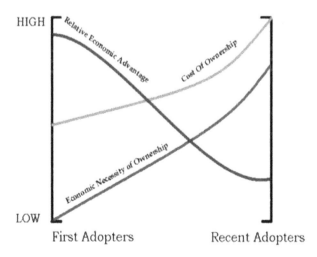

Figure 4.2 Economic Advantages of Snowmobile Relative to Costs. *Source*: Pelto and Müller-Wile (1972: 192).

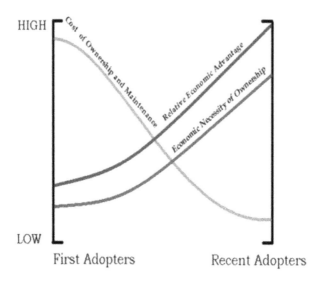

Figure 4.3   Economic Advantages of Mobile Phones Relative to Costs in Morocco.
Source: Pelto and Müller-Wile (1972: 192).

snowmobiles or trucks, as the direct costs of mobile phone ownership keeps decreasing, there has, at the same time, been an increase in their relative economic advantage and economic necessity of ownership. Moreover, mobile phones are inexpensive, require low maintenance and minimal energy, do not need expensive spare parts, , and connect people not only to their immediate places, as do trucks and snowmobiles, but to the rest of the country and the world as well. As a result, both the initial capital investment and continued operation of mobile phones are well within reach of many people and, unlike capital intensive forms of mechanized transportation and agriculture, they are not likely to lead to social and economic stratification; that stratification in the digital age is rather between areas inside and outside network coverage.

It is not simply the cost of investment that is at issue. A more important effect is at work here. With many old and non-networked technologies, the competitive advantage bestowed by an investment decreases as others in a system adopt a similar technology. Several studies on the effects of the "Green Revolution" in Asia, for instance, suggest that large farmers with early access to Green Revolution technologies (improved seeds, farm mechanization, irrigation technology, fertilizers, etc.) were able to outproduce and outcompete the non-adopters, in many cases driving small farmers and tenants out of business and purchasing their land (Griffin, 1972, 1974; Cleaver 1972). New technology led to lower product prices, higher input prices, and efforts by large-scale farmers to increase rents or force tenants off the land and attempts by big operators to increase landholdings by purchasing small farms, resulting in rural landless and rural outmigration, mostly to urban slums. These studies argued that the Green Revolution, although successful in terms of increasing food production and land areas utilizing the new technology, encouraged needless mechanization, creating a reduction in rural employment. The end product, they argue, was a quick increase in the inequality of income and asset distribution, and a worsening of poverty in areas affected by the Green Revolution technologies.

With mobile phones, something different happens. In the case of ICTs, the value of the investment depends directly on the number of other users. As Ethernet inventor Robert Metcalfe observed in the early 1990s, the value of networks increases exponentially with the addition of new participants in a networked medium. The relative economic advantage of ownership increases as other participants in an economic system acquire the technology. With a slight twist on the debate on common resources use (Ostrom 1990; Ilahiane 1999) and "the tragedy of the commons" (Hardin 1968), access and use of network does not lead to resource depletion or overuse, rather, the resource or the network is increased with each use; thus, enabling users to reap the rewards of the network effects.

CONCLUSION

It is evident from the earlier discussion that mobile phones are opportunity multipliers, and their effects have been profound in all areas of farming as well as other aspects of culture. Mobile phones have sped up ways in which farmers access market information and interact with market systems. They have enabled farmers to rework and leverage key cultural and religious concepts to take risks and intensify market participation. They have also empowered farmers to reorganize and pioneer new production and marketing strategies—and in some cases cut out middlemen from the agricultural supply chain—leading to higher farming revenues. Mobiles allowed famers to level the playing field of market information asymmetry, and in the process, they were empowered to make the transition from being information poor to information rich. In so doing, they enhanced their access to price information, far above and beyond farm gate prices, and have improved their terms of bargaining and the balance of power vis-à-vis middlemen. Of course, the effects of the mobile phone cannot be taken in isolation but must be considered in relation to the availability of network coverage, reliable transportation, postharvest storage facilities, and other agriculture and irrigation technologies.

Chapter 5

The Makings of Shame, Gender, and Place

The Mobile Phone Is Satan Number 71

In this chapter, I examine how Moroccans use mobile phones as a way of redefining issues of gender, honor, shame, and placemaking. I argue that mobile communication enables distance, becoming an invaluable vehicle for inverting and suspending ordinary gender roles and placemaking practices. Specifically, I claim that mobile phones allow users to switch the gender identity of the person on the other end of the call when they find themselves in a location where they must yield to certain cultural and religious norms and users deploy gender switching to maintain social order, which is anchored in that place. I also argue that mobile phones are not just objects but are in themselves "things" and constitute multi-vectored places.

There is a large body of literature on the effects and impacts of mobile technologies on time and space (Wilken and Goggin 2012; Ilahiane and Sherry 2012; Ito et al. 2011; Wilken 2011; Light 2011; Ling and Campbell 2011; Horst and Miller 2006;). Ling and Campbell (2011) argue that mobile communications have fundamentally changed how people experience distance and how they experience place or location. They write, "Mobile communication has meant that we call specific individuals, not general places" (2011, 2). Ito et al. (2011) describe mobile phones as a form of "cocooning" technology because they allow users to experience personalized media ecology that is carried around by the person rather than being hitched to a physical place. Mobile phone users at home are as copresent with intimate friends as are train passengers using a mobile phone who are potentially connected with others who are not geographically present. Similarly, Light (2011) argues that call recipients on the move lose themselves in phone conversations and create various mental spaces based on the context of their telephone use. Since phone users are calling people, and are not calling specific locations, Light suggests that "interlocutors caught in the wrong place tend to 'fill in' the image of the location and activities of the person on the other end of the call" (2011, 11). Hjort and Arnold argue that "place in its complexity has always mattered to mobile media . . . [and] mobile technology has eroded the importance and centrality of distance and location and has eased our detachment from places as complementing physical mobility" (2013, 19). Özkul points out that mobile technologies enable people to move freely by "freeing us from fixed lines and cables, and therefore from places . . . and they have the potential to influence what a place represents and embodies for its inhabitants" (2017, 6). Within the context of Morocco, Maroon (2006), Bowen et al. (2008), Kriem (2009), and Menin (2018) argue that mobile phone use has not only recalibrated the gender and sociality dynamics of communication in and outside the home but also equipped users with new ways to evade the religious and cultural taboos associated with sexual behavior without explicitly breaking them. And yet, amid this literature, there is less work on how mobile communications reengage such culture core concepts as gender, honor, and shame, and presence and placemaking.

In this chapter, I begin by focusing on mobile phone usage as it is structured through the Islamic principle of *khalwa* and the code of honor and shame. In revisiting Bourdieu's seminal analysis of the Berber Kabyle house, I seek to situate the use of mobile phones within the domestic practices of gender fluidity. I also reconsider Bourdieu's classic structural analysis of the Berber Kabyle house to argue that mobile phone users are not only switching the gender identity of the person on the end of the call when caught on the phone in a Berber house with a person of the opposite sex, but they are also having to go to great lengths to make sure that the Berber house remains a one-dimensional patriarchical domain. I also claim that mobile phones enable users to connect with people-in-place and not just people.

THE MOBILE PHONE, SHAME, AND DOMESTIC SPACE

The telephone occupies an intriguing place in Muslim societies. In Arabic, the word *hatif* means telephone and it is used for both fixed and mobile phones. People in the Middle East and North Africa distinguish between two types of telephony: mobile phones called *hatif jawals* or *hatif naqqals* (Arabic terms that literally mean telephones that are roaming, moving, or traveling around (masculine)); and fixed land lines called *hawateef thaabita* (Arabic terms that literally mean fixed telephones). Colloquially, in the Middle East, mobile phones are referred to simply by the Arabized English term *al-moobile*, and in North Africa, by the Arabized French term *al-portable*. The word *hatif* carries several meanings: "calling loudly from afar"; "unseen man whose voice is heard"; "a voice coming from an idol"; "an audible voice without possessing a visible body"; "an invisible caller"; and a "mysterious voice" (Wehr 1979, 1193; Larson 2011). According to Arab and Islamic stories, Iblis (the devil) disguised as the *hatif* (in this instance, meaning the caller), tempted Ali, Prophet Mohammad's son-in-law, ineffectively trying to stop him from ritually washing Prophet Mohammad's dead body.

With the availability of mobile phones, it has become easier to connect and socialize with individuals with whom one has no kinship relationship. Thus, the use of the mobile phone has challenged, if not eroded, the effectiveness of the principle of *khalwa*. In Islamic theology, the doctrine of *khalwa* demands that individuals outside a *mahram* relationship, meaning people one is not related to by marriage or blood ties should have no contact with each other. This doctrine is significant in Islamic debates on gender and sex roles on- and off-line. In a Sunni Muslim context that spares no effort to establish strict boundaries between the sexes, the mobile phone is viewed as a menacing technology because it enables users to come into contact with the opposite sex and to break the established norms of gendered spaces.

In addition to the Islamic doctrine of *khalwa*, other ideological conventions of gender and sex are framed and reinforced within the code of honor and shame. The code of honor and shame denotes a feeling, a state of consciousness and a set of individualistic and collective behaviors or practices rooted in a repertoire of patriarchal and religious beliefs. Delaney (1987) notes that the code of honor and shame "covers a variety of terms, meanings, and practices" that can be thought of as a "kind of genetic code—a structure of relations—generative of possibilities" (1987, 35). Abu-Lughod (1987) refers to honor, known in Arabic as *al-sharaf*, as a "network of honor-linked values," which include freedom from domination; self-reliance and autonomy; self-control; loyalty to kin and friends; keeping one's word; tough manliness; fearlessness; pride; and generosity. *Hshuma* (or `*ayb*) in Arabic means shame, but it also means to show respect (*waqar*), honorable modesty, subdued femininity, and deference to one's elders and social superiors. A family becomes ashamed when a member is involved in improper conduct. Much of the improper comportment is understood as being of a sexual nature. A dishonorable man is one whose lifestyle suggests loose morality. A woman, who goes out alone at night without the company of her relatives and carries out face-to-face or phone conversations with strangers, can be seen as scandalous and untrustworthy.

With the rapid uptake of mobile technologies throughout the Islamic world such as the mobile phone and other internet platforms (Facebook, WhatsApp, Skype, chat rooms, etc.), the doctrine of *khalwa* is also applied to regulating contact with the opposite sex in cyberspace. Al-Qarradawi, a prominent Sunni Muslim scholar who had a popular show on the Qatari-funded Al-Jazeera Network, argues that the justification behind gender separation and the banning of contact with the opposite sex "is not a lack of trust in one or both of them; it is rather to protect them from wrong thoughts and sexual feelings which naturally arise within a man and a woman when they are alone together without the fear or intrusion by a third-party person" (quoted in Larson 2011, 30). In his view, the doctrine of *khalwa* covers mobile phone calls and texts, and for that matter any other technology-mediated communications, and therefore these communications should be limited to necessary and emergency contacts and should exclude non-*mahram* contacts. The ability of mobile phone users to connect and establish *invisible* contact with strangers—anywhere, anytime—has elevated concerns about the old and traditional stability of gendered spaces. The presence of the mobile phone has made it hard to support the rules of *khalwa* and the code of honor and shame. At the same time, it has made it much easier for users to get involved in "veiled" or secret romantic relationships and adventures, flirt, or even date outside the edicts of the code of honor and shame and without the approval of patriarchical authority.

As one male laborer put it,

Since 1990 to now, shame (*al-`ayb*) has consisted of the use of the mobile phone and [its use by] women who lack certainty in their hearts (*yaqeen*) for God. One man I know divorced his wife because he caught her chatting on the mobile phone with someone. Loose morals and corrupting ways (*mafasid*) of the mobile are greater than its benefits (*masalih*). It must be banned. . . . You must know that, as we say, there are 70 Satans between a man and a woman and the mobile is number 71. . . . And before the coming of the mobile, do you know who Satan is? Satan is the thread (*al-kheet*, [meaning cable]) of satellite television dishes that sneaks from the roof into the hearth of people's houses. The cable is Satan, and it brings *mafasid* that only God could know, and no one can control that.

This ethnographic vignette exposes the complex ways that gender, morality, and place sit in relation to mobile phones and satellite television dishes. This is hardly surprising considering the moral panics that mobile technology has created inside and outside the domestic space. In Islam, female modesty marks the boundary between honor and shame; in public spaces, women behave in a reserved manner. Dating, as practiced in the West, does not exist in most North African societies, although young men and women are known to go to great lengths to meet in out-of-the-way places. Premarital sexuality is firmly controlled and legally sanctioned. Unlike women for whom virginity is required at the time of their weddings, men tend to have greater sexual freedom; it is not usually required of them to be a virgin at their wedding ceremonies (Flueher-Lobban 2004).

Writing on the Kabyle Berbers of Algeria, Bourdieu locates the issue of gender and sexuality dynamics within wider social and spatial relations and in the context of rules, customs, and taboos associated with the code of honor and shame. "Honor," writes Bourdieu, "is the basis of the moral code of an individual who sees himself always through the eyes of others, who has need of others for his existence, because the image he has of himself is indistinguishable from that presented to him by other people" (1966, 211). Thus, the dynamics of social honor take place within a setting invested with social exchanges consisting of a series of challenges and ripostes. Kabyles identify two reinforcing forms of honor: *nif* or the male point of honor and female *hurma*, which is sacred and off-limits to non-family members. *Hurma* defines roles and spatial positions of women within Berber society. *Hurma* also deals with femininity, "The sacred of the left hand—sexuality, privacy, magic, and food—*nif* with the sacred of the right hand—masculinity, and activities involving public life, political exchanges, and religion" (1966, 222). For Bourdieu, proper female behavior and the privacy of the family are crucial structural elements in the shaping of gender and sex roles.

In a corresponding article, Bourdieu provides a structuralist analysis of the Berber house in which he explores issues related to how gendered spaces reflect status and power differentials between men and women and suggests that the code of honor and shame is inscribed into the built environment. He also makes the claim that architecture shapes and maintains private and public social relations as spatial ideologies. Bourdieu notes, "A vision of the world is the division of the world" (1990a, 210). He argues that each division of the house is associated with rights according to a set of a series of balanced binary oppositions: "high/low, light/dark, day/night, male/female, *nif/hurma*, fertilizing/able to be fertilized" (1990b, 275). This spatial division reflects a division of the world into male and female spaces. In contrast to the male public sphere and farm labor, the domestic space of women "is *haram*, that is to say, both sacred and illicit for any man who is not part of it" (1990b, 275). Bourdieu writes,

> The house, a microcosm organized by the same oppositions and homologies that order the whole universe, stands in a relation of homology to the rest of the universe. But, from another standpoint, the world of the house, taken as a whole, stands in a relation of opposition to the rest of the world, an opposition whose principles are none other than those that organize both the internal space of the house and the rest of the world and, more generally, all areas of existence. (1990b, 277)

Bourdieu accepts the importance of binary oppositions that order the world of female life and the public world of men and claims that these opposing spatial areas ensure the social and economic viability of patriarchy. Hence, built environments are places of intense dialectical relationships between materiality and things in the context of such ideological conventions as honor and shame. As Bourdieu writes, "The most successful ideological effects are those which have no need of words and ask no more than complicitous silence" (1977, 188). Placemaking constitutes one of the most effective ideological effects. It appears that Bourdieu, while he was obviously writing within the structuralist tradition and before the advent of the mobile phone, was susceptible to the sense of containment and enclosure that such social categories as honor and shame imposed on the notion of place in Algeria, despite the long presence of French colonialism and the introduction of other "old" technologies such as radios, bicycles, mopeds, and cars. Bourdieu's approach to the Berber house assumed place—and therefore placemaking— was bounded and fixed by norms of patriarchy, and by extension, Islamic doctrines. But what if the Berber house is permeable, and involves invisible mobile phone callers whose ideas and interests conflict with the injunctions of the code of honor and shame and the law of *khalwa*? How do we make sense of this present-day patriarchal Berber house?

THE MOBILE PHONE AND GENDER AGILITY

The ethnographic vignette in the prior section tells of the satellite dish cable sneaking into the Berber house. The thread or cable is referred to as Satan because of what it is bringing into the house; the house that everyone thought was a sealed and sacred abode is now under siege from global satellite programming, not least of which features *haram* films whose provenance is mysterious and strange. Respondents recalled memories of kissing scenes or intimate moments appearing in films while watching television at home and how everyone had to scramble for cover, as it were, and look for something else to do. To contain the effects of shameful and improper ideas associated with un-Islamic material on television, the patriarch at home would, in most cases, turn off the television or ask family members to close their eyes or look away until the scene passed or to leave the television area altogether. In other cases, the patriarch and the family members would just pretend to be doing something else until the scene passed. In this context, non-roaming technologies such as satellite dishes could be controlled and patriarchal morality and honor and shame order maintained, even when it was clearly breached and everyone involved felt ashamed and vulnerable to external forces.

With the introduction of the mobile phone, something drastically different occurs. The mobile phone is "a lot of places and a lot of people" and because of its networked capabilities, not unlike Wi-Fi hot spots, to roam invisibly, mingle along, through, and around other places, it has empowered users to come in and out of disparate places with ease, and sometimes with calculated discretion, smuggling themselves in and out of place, so to speak. In other words, mobile phones stalk places and their inhabitants. When asked about the use of the mobile phone for developing or maintaining romantic relationships, one electrician, surprised by the question about sexual relations, at first felt embarrassed to answer. Much later he would admit that much of the use of new technologies deals with romantic and sexual pursuits. After he felt comfortable with discussing romantic relationships, he said,

> The mobile phone is the best manner for developing a romantic adventure. The people of the house or the neighborhood do not know who you are talking to or involved with. You use it for meeting the person you are interested in and nobody knows. The mobile makes it easier. All you need is a phone number, and the mobile does the rest.

He goes on to say,

> If you were looking for a romantic partner . . . the mobile makes it easy to initiate and manage the relationship, but at the same time you have to be on guard all the time and you have to know where your mobile is. You see, I cannot just leave it anywhere or trust anyone with it.

I asked, "Why worry this much"? He responded, "The mobile is like hauling a thread with you all the time." I responded, "That allows you to stay on top of your relationships and movement at home, in the neighborhood, and in the city and wherever work might take you." He said, "All you said is correct but, look, the mobile is a trap too!" I inquired, "A trap! What does trap mean?" He responded,

> You see, during prayer time at home, you have to set it aside and you have to make sure that the people of the house do not know where it is or put it in silence because girlfriends may call. I should tell you that if you give your number to a girl and she calls you when you are at home, it is the essence of shame and awkwardness in front of the parents and my brothers and sisters. Last week, no, last month, a girlfriend called me, and I was at home. As you know, everyone can hear your conversation in our house, so I turned the girl into a man and kept talking. I did not want my father and my mother to know that I was talking to a girl. Several workers do the same, and women involved in premarital relations do the same and turn men into women when they call them in their houses.

What is remarkable about the aforementioned passage is the care that young men and women must take to preserve the patriarchal domain when they embark on potential romantic adventures. Because of the moral panic and perceived danger, they spare no effort to keep them secret and as far as possible from home and the neighborhood. Equally significant is the work that goes into the repair of the intrusion of mobile phones into the patriarchal dominion by forms of what I call gender switching to make sure that the patriarchal domain remains one-dimensional. In the context of a conversation and "creative sociability" to uphold traditional values and structures, one may actually in a fleeting moment switch the gender of the individual on the other end of the line, and in so doing, one may also be involved in amending, or even subverting, the rules of gendered space. Indeed, several authors have explored the moral panics generated by mobile phone use in the developing world. Archambault (2012) found that the mobile phone in Mozambique is just as likely to become a tool for controlling women as for empowering them. She argues that the potential of the mobile phone to transform gender and power dynamics in the longer term remains to be seen. For instance, she cites one example of a husband who, while working away from home, uses his mobile phone to "check up" on his wife and make sure that she is actually at home. Anderson (2013) found that "phone friendships" enable women in Papua New Guinea to escape traditional cross-gender relations. Similarly, Doron argues that a woman's usage of the mobile phone in north India is "highly regulated by her husband and in-laws, but one that she is bound to have increasing access to as she rises in the household hierarchy over her life course" (2012, 430). What remains unconsidered in the literature on mobile communication and the transgression of gender boundaries, however, are the ways in which mobile phones allow users to switch the gender identity of the person to whom they are speaking quickly when they find themselves in a location where they must adhere to the cultural and religious norms of that place.

In other words, gender switching allows individuals to restore the status quo between the sexes and to insulate patriarchal morality from external threats. At the same time, however, mobile phone users know that to shield the foundations of patriarchy and honor, to preserve their "creative sociability," and to avoid antagonizing them with a spatial and social reality they find limiting, it remains necessary for everyone involved to preserve appearances. The deployment of gender switching is an instance of a productive drive toward order within a social reality fraught with mutually exclusive and incommensurable cultural forms and spatial practices, or what Whitaker (2016) calls "amiable incoherence." The pressures of "amiable incoherence" produce the deployment of momentary gender switching and *déplacement* into a networked oasis of conversation. There the dichotomization of social and spatial forms is provisionally suspended, and phone users carve up a sort of an oasis/hot spot form of going-out sociability, without actually exiting the spatial confines of the Berber House. This oasis/hot spot is the site where opposed social and spatial forms of life are given a quick and transitory fix, and it is a crossroad of intimate, private, and public spaces, defined by creative sociability; it is the place where the world is permeable (cf. Bourdieu 1990b).

One of the laborers in my study kept referring to the mobile phone as Satan number 71. The description of the mobile phone as Satan number 71 is pertinent and in many ways captures the angst over its invisible force to penetrate fixed places and to revise their social and spatial boundaries. In a Muslim context, the word Satan conveys the idea of rebellion and enmity. Satan is of the *Jinn*, a species of living beings, meaning a spirit, or an invisible or hidden force possessing a certain amount of free will. It also denotes the idea of evil from all sides tempting men and women to commit improper behavior. In Islamic theology, Satan deceived Adam and Eve and made them eat from the forbidden tree. Adam and Eve felt shame and God removed them from Paradise and made them dwell on earth (Ali 1999). In our case, however, it seems that the mobile phone was put into a mode of creative sociability that took the form of fleeting moments of gender switching and *déplacement* while still in place—a place hemmed in by religious and social restrictions. The mobile phone users did not feel completely ashamed and were not removed from their networked oasis/hot spot, so to speak. Hence, in this context, how do we define place in the age of the mobile phone?

A MOBILE PHONE IS A THING
AND A PLACE IS A KNOT

Several scholars from different disciplinary backgrounds have investigated the notions of space and place. Lefebvre (1991) argues that spaces are not always containers of social and cultural production, but rather they are organized by cultural codes and symbolic meanings. He contends that space is always in a state of becoming. Similarly, Ingold (2000), whose writings and theorizing on place are derived from Lefebvre (1991) and Heidegger (1977), argues against the binary opposition categories of culture versus nature, which suggest a clear-cut separation between the built and non-built environments and takes issue with the notion that people have produced their cultural milieus from an empty natural space. Ingold writes that "something . . . must be wrong somewhere if the only way to understand our creative involvement in the world is by taking ourselves out of it." Rather he states that people are part and parcel of nature, and they are also "in the world" (2000, 173).

He puts forward Heidegger's notion of dwelling, which refers to "the forms people build, whether in the imagination or on the ground, arise within the current of their involved activity, in the specific relational contexts of their practical engagement with their surroundings" (2000, 186). He suggests that people are involved in their environments, not as outsiders but as constituents of them. Furthermore, Ingold (2010) argues against the containment and enclosure that social scientists attach to the concept of place, as in the case of Bourdieu mentioned earlier. Ingold writes, "A place is a meshwork. . . . Lives are not led inside places but through, around, to and from them, from and to places elsewhere, human experience unfolds not in places but along paths . . . places, then are like knots" (2010, 13). In other words, any given place is dependent on its mutually constituent parts and is also dependent on its connectedness with other places. This also articulates the point that places are susceptible to permeability, which may bring about their dissolution or trigger their evolution.

From this perspective, places mingle with each other and are understood as bounded but open and engaged in dialectics of power, freedom, and control. Ingold posits that places are caught up in multiple entanglements through which "the built environment is more archi-textural than architectural (Lefebvre 1991, 117–118)" (Ingold chapter 2, 34). Similarly, Massey refers to these social and spatial dynamics as "the thrown togetherness" of place, the "event" of place (2005, 181). In this context, my ethnographic analysis of the Moroccan house demonstrates the entanglement of mobile phones, cultural and religious codes, and domestic and public places, both on the ground and on the mobile phone, are never circumscribed places but are always in a state of flux and movement. The mobile phone "gathers everything," is "a lot of places and a lot of people," and in the words of Ingold, it embodies the notion of it being a "thing" rather than an object. Based on Heidegger's distinction between objects and things, Ingold writes:

> The object stands before us as a *fait accompli*, presenting its congealed, outer surfaces to our inspection. It is defined by its very "overagainstness" in relation to the setting in which it is placed (Heidegger 1971, 167). The thing, by contrast, is a "going on," or better, a place where several goings on become entwined. To observe a thing is not to be locked out but to be invited into the gathering. We participate, as Heidegger rather enigmatically put it, in the thing' thinging in a worlding world. . . . The thing has the character not of an externally bounded entity, set over and against the world, but of a knot whose constituent threads, far from being contained within it, trail beyond, only to become caught with other threads in other knots. Or in a word, things leak, forever discharging through the surfaces that form temporarily around them. (2010, 4)

Within this lens, the mobile phone exceeds its objecthood, and it is "a place laborers go to," "a place that brings work," a saint, a shrine, a mosque, a café, a soccer pitch on the beach, a watching and surveillance area, a reputation, a *qibla* (direction), an invisible agent or *jinn*, a feeling, an emotion, and a short-lived romantic parking spot. It is where locations meet and crisscross each other and move on to other things. These "lots of places and lots of people" stalk other places they happen to encounter, and in the process, they shape and are shaped by these places too. The mobile phone meddling, while emanating from a powerful and invisible origin, has the capability to run through, around, and along spatial and social checkpoints with ease, yet it must yield to the prescriptions of the code of honor and shame and religious injunctions. This caving in which takes the form of gender switching, however, allows for the stretching of time, and at the same time, gives a new lease of life to the ideological conventions governing patriarchy and the doctrine of *khalwa*. With the mobile phone, there are no far-reaching ruptures of the social and the spatial; there are only slits that can be quickly stitched. In this context, my findings confirm to a certain extent the insight of Ito et al. (2011), which states that mobile phones stitch various places and cover a heterogeneous set of social, geographical, and spatial contexts, leading to the formation of what they call cocooning. In my case, cocooning occurs, but it takes the form of gender switching in the context of a conversation oasis that callers perceive as a danger to the logic of patriarchy and the code of honor and shame and deploy gender switching to shield the status quo from further and deeper disruptions instigated by the continuous mingling and movement of places and people.

CONCLUSION

Mobile phones, like other technologies before them, have *revealed* other aspects of the Berber house in a way that shows that it is not exempt from external threats and influences. Mobile phone connectivity demonstrates, once again, that our dwellings, whether imagined or on the ground, represent unpredictable physical and social locations and provide other possibilities for making better sense of these dwellings. In contrast to Wellman's claims that "mobile phone connectivity has ushered in the age of networked individualism in which individuals are enabled to connect to people and not to places . . . and in which 'physical context becomes less important'" (2002, 5), mobile phones, upon encountering the Berber house, reveal how distance shapes location and gender roles on the fly in fundamental ways. In using mobile phones, while Moroccans cannot extricate themselves from honor and shame obligations, which sit in the Berber house, they are empowered to quickly reverse gender roles on the phone, which, in turn, transforms the phone itself into a shielded location of an otherwise shared domestic space. Moreover, in revealing fleeting moments of gender reversal and the relevance of location, mobile phones succeed in not only affirming ordinary social and spatial context but also exposing location and its moral demarcations as fundamentally unpredictable, volatile sites—where people still do connect with people-in-places.

Conclusion

The central argument of this book is that the mobile phone is a total social artifact which has co-shaped and transformed preexisting cultural, social, and economic systems. In fact, the mobile phone, a product as well as a driver of globalization, has revised established social and economic conditions and ushered in a new socio-technical environment where such core concepts as place, time, information, market, sociality, work, and religion have been reworked and, in the process, were transvalued by the connectivity aspect of mobile telephony. As the embodiment of globalization, I argue that the mobile phone does not only constitute one of the central elements of globalization but also involves almost all elements of globalization. In fact, given the myriad ways in which the mobile phone has transformed every aspect of social life, the term *mobile phone* appears insufficient to capture the surplus activities of this technological object. The mobile phone is not just an object used for talking but is itself a thing, a thing imbued with beliefs and values and composed of various technological properties such as always-on connectivity, a simple computer, camera, music and game player, personal scheduler, alarm clock, and calculator (Brown 2001; Ingold 2010).

The thingness properties of the mobile phone share similarities with Appadurai's framework of globalization, which is composed of five specific "scapes" or flows: ethnoscapes (flows of people across boundaries); technoscapes (flows of technology); ideoscapes (flows of ideas across borders); financescapes (flows of money across political borders); and mediascapes (flows of media content across borders). As Appadurai writes, "Technology, both high and low, both mechanical and informational, now moves at high speeds across various kinds of previously impervious boundaries" (1996, 34). Conceptualizing globalization in terms of things, people, and ideas that flow across national boundaries is a productive framework for making sense of the ways in which the mobile phone object/thing has transformed social and economic landscapes that frame daily life. While the five scapes defined by Appadurai provide a useful framework to think through these global flows, separating them in this way can be incomplete because the mobile phone phenomenon brings together all these flows. In this book, I demonstrated the economic productivity of mobile phone users, as well as the social and cultural challenges facing them in a Muslim context. I addressed men and women's practices and everyday-life engagements of mobile phones in a variety of economic and cultural settings, while, at the same time, showing how these men and women responded to technological and social transformations and challenges. The urban street vendors, urban micro-entrepreneurs, urban female domestic workers, and smallholder farmers that were presented in this book were affected economically and socially by their engagement with mobile phones.

I addressed the informal economy of the world of the mobile phone urban street vendor and the vast pool of entrepreneurial vigor that was ready to engage the use of the mobile phone. I showed how urban micro-entrepreneurs and female domestic workers use the mobile phone as a tool to organize a networked work life, and how mobile phone use expanded the productive opportunities of certain types of activities by enhancing social networks, reducing risks associated with employment seeking, and enabling freelance service work, leading to income increases. I examined the use of mobile phones by farmers and demonstrated how mobile telephony has deepened market participation, resulting in intensive cultivation of cash crops, higher farming revenues, and recalibration of market information flows and terms. I investigated how Moroccans use mobile phones as a way of reframing issues of gender, honor, and shame, and placemaking, and I showed that mobile phones are "things" and not just simple objects. Finally, throughout the book, I demonstrated how Moroccan men and women have been successful in infusing mobile phones with their economic, social, cultural, and religious beliefs, meanings, ethos, and practices, and in the process, they made mobile phones fit their contexts.

I am aware that the domains of social and economic change addressed in my book are limited to the economic productivity of mobile phones and the rearrangement of some key cultural and religious obligations and concepts. This is far from a comprehensive catalog of domains of change brought about by the mobile phone and the rise of the network society, especially in the domain of collective political mobilization and change (McLuhan 1971; Sreberny-Mohammadi and Mohammadi 1994; Eickelman and Anderson 1999; Rheingold 2002; Diani and McAdam 2003; Castells 2007; Liu 2017). Undoubtedly, the impressive adoption of the mobile phone in conjunction with the availability of social media applications have invigorated and sustained local and global movements for human rights and social justice, such as the pro-democracy uprisings of the Arab Spring that began in 2010–2011 (Ilahiane 2011, 2017, 2019; Rachik 2016; Bayat 2017; Bennani-Chraïbi 2021). While the political dimension of the mobile phone is one of the topics that fall outside of the scope of the present study, it is important for future ethnographic studies to consider the implications of mobile phone use for collective political action, especially in political contexts that lack transparent political parties, professional associations, and a free press to articulate people's grievances and make demands for change; and its capacity in crafting bottom-up paths for transitions toward viable livelihoods and freedom from political oppression in a world mired in ever-increasing economic injustice and political humiliation.

In short, the growing body of non-ethnographic work (Masbah 2018; Echine 2019) exploring how mobile phones and social media platforms affect political action in Morocco (i.e., the "Let it-Spoil" boycott campaign and the Rif Movement) seems to suggest that these new technologies have not only played an important role of counterinformation and correcting the government version of political reality but also succeeded in the formation of what Moroccan internet users call casually, "The Political Party of Facebook." Within this setting, mobile phones appear to have enabled users to mainstream their marginal voices and enforce their visions of society on national politics, and at the same time, granted themselves augmented access to local and nonlocal spaces to engage in "the practice of freedom," defined by Freire as "the means by which men and women deal critically and creatively with reality and discover how to participate in the transformation of their world" (1973, 34).

If this ethnographic account could accomplish one thing, I hope that it provides a deeper sense of how the mobile phone has mobilized, translocalized, transvalued, and transformed almost every facet of Moroccan life. My point of departure in this book was my claim that the mobile phone is a total social artifact which assembles Mauss' notion of total social fact and Latour's ANT. Based on the analysis outlined through different domains of activity, I see the mobile phone not just as a simple object but as a thing in itself where sociotechnical processes are at work, one that further pushes the boundaries of how anthropologists understand notions of culture, economy, place, time, and the global-local dynamics transforming them. The mobile phone is part of a system of ideas, a way of being in the world, and a way of seeing and acting on the world. For most Moroccans, however, it is a liberation thing where users and technology come together to engage and animate each other; and I argue that through these human-nonhuman entanglements, this technology-thing has assisted Moroccans in designing alternative lifeways and livelihoods that join the local and the nonlocal. This can be seen in the stories and experiences of the street vendors, micro-entrepreneurs, domestic workers, and farmers, who participated in this study and how their worlds have been transformed in a variety of ways by the introduction and use of the mobile phone. In the words of Illich (1973), the mobile phone thing is "a tool for conviviality," meaning that it is enabling and strengthening people's capacity to aspire for designing futures of dignity, autonomy, solidarity, and prosperity.

Bibliography

Abu-Lughod, L. 1987. *Veiled Sentiments: Honor and Poetry in a Bedouin Society*. Berkeley, CA: University of California Press.

Agence Nationale de Réglementation des Télécommunications (ANRT). 2018. *Le Rapport Annuel 2018*. Rabat, Morocco: ARNT. Retrieved July 28, 2019. http://www.anrt.ma/fr/admin/download/upload/file_fr1525.pdf.

———. 2007. *Le Rapport Annuel 2007*. Retrieved July 28, 2008. http://www.anrt.ma/fr/admin/download/upload/file_fr1525.pdf

Aker, Jenny. 2011. "Dial "A" for Agriculture: A Review of Information and Communication Technologies for Agricultural Extension in Developing Countries." *Agricultural Economics* 42, no. 2: 631–647.

———. 2008. *Does Digital Divide or Provide? The Impact of Cell Phones on Grain Markets in Niger*. Center for Global Development working paper No. 154. Retrieved September 15, 2020. SSRN. http://ssrn.com/abstract=1093374.

Akrich, Madeleine. 1992. "The Description of Technical Objects." In *Shaping Technology/Building Society: Studies in Sociotechnical Change*, edited by Wiebe Bijker and John Law, 205–225. Cambridge, MA: The MIT Press.

Ali, Abdullah. 1999. *The Meaning of the Holy Qur'an*. Beltsville, MD: Amana Publications.

Ames, Morgan. 2019. *The Charismatic Machine: The Life, Death, and Legacy of One Laptop Per Child*. Cambridge, MA: The MIT Press.

———. 2015. "Charismatic Technology." In *Proceedings of the Fifth Decennial Aarhus Conference on Critical Alternatives*, chaired by Olav W. Bertelsen, Kim Halskov, Shaowen Bardzell, and Ole Iversen, 109–120, Aarhus University Press.

Anderson, Barbara. 2013. "Tricks, Lies, and Mobile Phones: 'Phone Friend' Stories in Papua New Guinea." *Culture, Theory and Critique*, 11, no. 3: 318–334.

Appadurai, Arjun. 1996. *Modernity at Large: Cultural Dimensions of Globalization*. Minneapolis, MN: University of Minnesota Press.

Archambault, Julie. 2017. *Mobile Secrets: Youth, Intimacy, and the Politics of Pretense in Mozambique*. Chicago: University of Chicago Press.

———. 2012. "Mobile Phones and the "Commercialization" of Relationships: Expressions of Masculinity in Southern Mozambique." In *Gender and Modernity in Global Youth Cultures,* edited by Susan Dewey and Karren Bison, 47–71. Syracuse: Syracuse University Press.

———. 2011. "Breaking up "because of the phone' and the Transformative Potential of Information in Southern Mozambique." *New Media & Society* 13: 444–456.

Arora, Payal. 2019. *The Next Billion Users: Digital Life beyond the West.* Cambridge, MA: Harvard University Press.

———. 2016. *Dot Com Mantra: Social Computing in the Central Himalayas.* London: Routledge.

Bayat, Asef. 2017. *Revolutions Without Revolutionaries: Making Sense of the Arab Spring.* Palo Alto, CA: Stanford University Press.

Bennani-Chraïbi, Mounia. 2021. *Partis politiques et protestations au Maroc (1934-2020).* Rennes, France: Presses universitaires de Rennes.

Bogaert, Koenraad. 2018. *Globalized Authoritarianism: Megaprojects, Slums, and Class Relations in Urban Morocco.* Minneapolis, MN: University of Minnesota Press.

Bohannan, Paul, ed. 1962. *Markets in Africa.* Evanston, IL: Northwestern University Press.

Bourdieu, Pierre. 1990a. *The Logic of Practice.* Cambridge, UK: Polity Press.

———. 1990b [1970]. The Berber House or the World Reversed. Appendix in *The Logic of Practice.* Cambridge, UK: Polity Press.

———. 1977. *Outline of a Theory of Practice.* Cambridge, UK: Cambridge University Press.

———. 1966. "The Sentiment of Honour in Kabyle Society." In *Honor and Shame: The Values of Mediterranean Society*, edited by Jean G. Peristiany, 193–241. Chicago: University of Chicago Press.

———. 1962. *The Algerians.* Boston, MA: Beacon Press.

Bowen, Donna, Alexia Green, and Christiann James. 2008. "Globalization, Mobile Phones and Forbidden Romance in Morocco." *Journal of North African Studies* 13, no. 2: 227–241.

Bowen, John. 2008. *Religions in Practice: An Approach to the Anthropology of Religion.* 4th edition. New York: Pearson Education, Inc.

Brey, Philip. 2005. "Artifacts as Social Agents." In *Inside the Politics of Technology*, edited by H. Harbers, pp. 61–84. Amsterdam: Amsterdam University Press.

Brown, Bill. 2001. "Thing Theory." *Critical Inquiry* 28, no. 1: 1–22.

Callon, Michel. 1987. "Society in the Making: The Study of Technology as a Tool for Sociological Analysis." In *The social Construction of Technological Systems: New Directions in the Sociology and History of Technology*, edited by T. Hughes and T. Pinch, 83–103. Cambridge, MA: MIT Press.

Callon, Michel, and Bruno Latour. 1992. "Don't Throw the Baby out with the Bath School! A Reply to Collins and Yearley." In *Science as Practice and Culture*, edited by A. Pickering, 343–368. Chicago, IL: University of Chicago Press.

Callon, Michel, John Law, and Arie Rip, eds. 1986. *Mapping the Dynamics of Science and Technology.* London, UK: Palgrave Macmillan.

Castells, Manuel. 2007. "Communication, Power, and Counter-power in the Network Society." *International Journal of Communication* 1: 238–266.

———. 1996. *The Rise of the Network Society*. Malden, MA: Blackwell Publishers.

Castells, Manuel, Mireia Fernandez-Ardevol, Jack Qiu, and Araba Sey. 2006. *Mobile Communication and Society: A Global Perspective*. Cambridge, MA: The MIT Press.

Castells, Manuel, and Alejandro Portes, eds. 1989. "World Underneath: The Origins, Dynamics, and Effects of the Informal Economy." In *The Informal Economy*, edited by Manuel Castells and Alejandro Portes, 11–17. Baltimore, MD: Johns Hopkins University Press.

Chatty, Dawn. 1996. *Mobile Pastoralists: Development and Planning Social Change in Oman*. New York: Columbia University Press.

Chickering, Lawrence, and Mohamed Salahdine, eds. 1991. *The Silent Revolution: The Informal Sector in Five Asian and Near Eastern Countries*. San Francisco, CA: ICS Press.

Christensen, Clayton. 2000. *The Innovator's Dilemma*. New York: Harper Collins Publishers.

Çizakça, Murat. 2000. *A History of Philanthropic Foundations: The Islamic World from the Seventh Century to the Present*. Istanbul: Bogazici University Press.

Cleaver, Harry. 1972. "The Contradictions of the Green Revolution." *American Economic Review* 62:177–88.

Costa, Elizabetta. 2019. "Location as Conspicuous Consumption: The Making of Modern Women and Consumer Culture in south-east Turkey." In *Location technologies in International Context*, edited by Rowan Wilken, Gerard Goggin, and Heather A. Horst, 43–53. London: Routledge.

———. 2016. *Social Media in Southeast Turkey*. London: UCL Press.

Crewe, Emma, and Richard Axelby. 2013. *Anthropology and Development: Culture, Morality and Politics in a Globalized World*. Cambridge, UK: Cambridge University Press.

Dalton, George. 1971. *Economic Anthropology and Development: Essays on Tribal and Peasant Economies*. New York: Basic Books.

Delany, Carol. 1987. "Seeds of Honor, Fields of Shame." In *Honor and Shame and Unity of the Mediterranean*, edited by David Gilmore, 35–48. Washington, DC: American Anthropological Association.

De Soto, Hernando. 2000. *The Mystery of Capital: Why Capitalism Triumphs in the West and Fails Everywhere Else*. New York: Basic Books.

———. 1987. *The Third Path: The Invisible Revolution in the Third World*, New York: Basic Books.

Diani, Mario, and Doug McAdam, eds. 2003. *Social Movements and Networks: Relational Approaches to Collective Action*. New York: Oxford University Press.

Donner, Jonathan. 2010. "Framing M4D: The Utility and Continuity and the Dual Heritage of 'Mobiles for Development.'" *The Electronic Journal on Information Systems in Developing Countries* 44, no. 3: 1–16.

———. 2009. "Blurring Livelihoods and Lives: The Social Uses of Mobile Phones and Socioeconomic Development." *Innovations* (winter): 91–100.

————. 2008. "Research Approaches to Mobile Use in the Developing World: A Review of the Literature." *The Information Society* 24, no. 3: 140–159.

————. 2006. "The Use of Mobile Phones by Microentrepreneurs in Kigali, Rwanda: Change to Social and Business Networks." *Information Technologies and International Development* 3, no. 2: 3–19.

Doron, Assa. 2012. "Mobile Persons: Cell Phones, Gender and the Self in North India." *The Asia Pacific Journal of Anthropology*, 13, no. 5: 414–433.

Doron, Assa, and Robin Jeffrey. 2013. *The Great Indian Phone Book: How the Cheap Cell Phone Changes Business, Politics, and Daily Life*. Cambridge, MA: Harvard University Press.

Durkheim, Emile. 2020 [1895]. "What Is a Social Fact?" In *Anthropological Theory: An Introductory History*, edited by R. Jon McGee and Richard L. Warms, 86–93. Lanham, MD: Rowman & Littlefield.

Echine, Ayyad. 2019. "Social Media and Social Mobility: Exploring the Role of Social Networks in the 2018 Boycott Campaign in Morocco." *Journal of Cyberspace Studies* 3, no. 1: 59–78.

Edgar, Andrew, and Peter Sedgwick, eds. 2002. "Cultural Anthropology." In *The Key Concepts*. New York: Routledge.

Eickelman, Dale. 2002. *The Middle East and Central Asia: An Anthropological Approach*. Fourth edition. Upper Saddle River, NJ: Prentice Hall.

Eickelman, Dale, and Jon Anderson, eds. 1999. *New Media in the Muslim World: The Merging Public Sphere*. Bloomington, IN: Indiana University Press.

Escobar, Arturo. 1995. *Encountering Development: The Making and Unmaking of the Third World*. Princeton, NJ: Princeton University Press.

Flueher-Lobban, Carolyn. 2004. *Islamic Societies in Practice*. Gainesville, FL: University Press of Florida.

Fortunati, Leopoldina. 2005. "Mobile Phones and Fashion in Post-modernity." *Telekronikk*, 3, no. 4: 35–48.

Foster, Robert, and Heather Horst, eds. 2018. *The Moral Economy of Mobile Phones: Pacific Islands Perspectives*. Canberra: ANU Press.

Freire, Paulo. 1973. *Pedagogy of the Oppressed*. New York: Continuum.

Gardner, Katy, and David Lewis. 2015. *Anthropology and Development: Challenges of the Twenty-First Century*. London: Pluto Press.

Geertz, Clifford. 1979. "Suq: The Bazaar Economy in Sefrou." In *Meaning and Order in Contemporary Morocco: Three Essays in Cultural Anthropology*, edited by Clifford Geertz, Hildred Geertz, and Lawrence Rosen, 123–225. New York: Cambridge University Press.

————. 1963. *Peddlers and Princes: Social Development and Economic Change in Two Indonesian Towns*, Chicago: University of Chicago Press.

Gellner, Ernest. 1969. *Saints of the Atlas*. Chicago: University of Chicago Press.

Ghanem, Hafez. 2015. *Agriculture and Rural Development for Inclusive Growth and Food Security in Morocco*. Global Economy and Development Working Paper 82. Washington, DC: The Brookings Institution.

Gittel, Ross, and Avis Vidal. 1998. *Community Organizing: Building Social Capital as a Development Strategy*. Thousand Oaks, CA: Sage Publications.

Glotz, Peter, Stefan Bertchi, and Chris Locke, eds. 2005. *Thumb Culture: The Meanings of Mobile Phones for Society.* New Brunswick, NJ: Transactions Publishers.

Goggin, Gerard. 2006. *Cell Phone Culture: Mobile Technology in Everyday Life.* New York: Routledge.

Goodman, David. 2005. *Linking Mobile Phone Ownership and Use to Social Capital in South Africa and Tanzania.* Retrieved July 9, 2008. http://www.vodafone.com /etc/medialib/attachments/cr_downloads.Par.78351.File.dat/GPP_SIM_paper_3 .pdf

Granovetter, Mark. 1973. "The Strength of Weak Ties." *American Journal of Sociology* 78, no. 6: 1360–1380.

Greenberg, James, and Thomas Park. 2017. *Hidden Interests in Credit and Finance.* Lanham, MD: Lexington Books.

Griffin, Keith. 1974. *The Political Economy of Agrarian Change.* London: Macmillan.

———. 1972. *The Green Revolution: An Economic Analysis.* Geneva: United Nations Research Institute for Social Development.

Hajji, Nasr. 2001. *Insertion du Maroc dans la société de l'information et du savoir: pour une nouvelle vision.* Casablanca, Afrique Orient.

Hammond, Allen, William Kramer, Julia Tran, and Courtland Walker. 2007. *The Next 4 Billion: Market Size and Business Strategy at the Base of the Pyramid.* Washington, DC: World Resources Institute.

Hammoudi, Abdellah. 1997. *Master and Disciple: The Cultural Foundations of Moroccan Authoritarianism.* Chicago: University of Chicago Press.

Hardin, G. 1968. "The Tragedy of the Commons." *Science* 162: 1243–1248.

Harper, Richard. 2003. "Are Mobiles Good or Bad for Society? In *Mobile Democracy: Essays on Society, Self and Politics*, edited by Kristof Nyı´ri, 185–214. Budapest, Hungary: Passagen Verlag.

Hart, Keith. 1973. "Informal Economy Opportunities and the Urban Employment in Ghana." *Journal of Modern Africa Studies* 11, no. 1: 61–89.

Harvey, David. 1990. *The Condition of Modernity: An Inquiry into the Origins of Culture Change.* Malden, MA: Blackwell Publishers.

Heidegger, Martin. 1996 [1927]. *Being and Time: A Translation of Sein Und Zeit.* Translated by Joan Stambaugh. Albany, NY: State University of New York Press.

———. 1977. *The Question Concerning Technology and Other Essays.* New York: Harper & Row.

———. 1971. "The Thing." In *Poetry, Language, Thought.* Translated by Albert Hofstadter. New York: Harper & Row.

Henry, M. Clement. 1996. The *Mediterranean Debt Crescent: Money and Power in Algeria, Egypt, Morocco, Tunisia, and Turkey.* Gainesville, FL: University of Florida Press.

Henry, M. Clement, and Robert Springborg. 2001. *Globalization and the Politics of Development in the Middle East.* New York: Cambridge University Press.

Hjort, Larissa, and Michael Arnold. 2013. *Online@AsiaPacific: Mobile, Social and Locative in the Asia-Pacific Region.* London: Routledge.

Horst, Heather. 2021. "The Anthropology of Mobile Phones." In *Digital Anthropology*, edited by Haidy Geismar and Hannah Knox, 65–84. London: Routledge.

Horst, Heather, and Daniel Miller. 2006. *The Cell Phone: An Anthropology of Communication*. New York: Berg.

———. 2005. "From Kinship to Link-up: Cell Phones and Social Networking in Jamaica." *Current Anthropology* 46, no. 5: 755–778.

Hottinger, Arnold. 1961. "Zu'ama and Parties in the Lebanese Crisis of 1958." *Journal of the Middle East* 15, no. 2: 127–140.

Ibahrine, Mohamed. 2004. "Towards a National Telecommunications Strategy in Morocco." *First Monday* 9, no. 1. http://firstmonday.org/issues/issue9_1/ibahrine/index.html

Ilahiane, Hsain. 2019. "Why Do Protests Keep Happening in North Africa? It is *al-hogra*." https://www.juancole.com/2019/01/protests-happening-africa.html

———. 2017. "Morocco's Rif Revolt: Only a Democratic Response is Sufficient." *Informed Comment*. https://www.juancole.com/2017/07/moroccos-democratic-sufficient.html

———. 2011. "Pro-democracy and Dignity Uprisings in North Africa and the Middle East." Committee on Human Rights and Social Justice Briefing 2. Society for Applied Anthropology. http://www.sfaa.net/committees/humanrights/HRSJIssueBriefing2.pdf

———. 2007. "Impacts of Information and Communication Technologies in Agriculture: Farmers and Mobile Phones in Morocco." Paper presented at the Annual Meetings of the American Anthropological Association. Washington, DC, December 1.

———. 2004. *Ethnicities, Community Making, and Agrarian Change: The Political Ecology of a Moroccan Oasis*. Lanham, MD: University Press of America.

———. 1999. "Berber *Agdal* Institution: Indigenous Range Management in the Atlas Mountains." *Ethnology* 1: 21–45.

Ilahiane, Hsain, and John Sherry. 2012. "The Problematics of the "Bottom of the Pyramid" Approach to International Development: The Case of Micro-entrepreneurs' Use of Mobile Phones in Morocco." *International Technologies and International Development* 8, no. 1: 13–26.

———. 2008. "Joutia: Street Vendor Entrepreneurship and the Informal economy of Information and Communication Technologies in Morocco." *Journal of North African Studies* 13, no. 2: 243–255.

———. 2004. "Mobile Phones, Globalization, and Productivity in Morocco." *In Information Technology, Globalization, and the Future*. Intel, Hillsboro, Oregon.

Ilahiane, Hsain and Marcie L. Venter. 2016. "Introduction: Technologies and the Transformation of Economies." *Economic Anthropology* 3, no. 2: 191–202.

Illich, Ivan. 1973. *Tools for Conviviality*. New York: Marion Boyars.

Ingold, Tim. 2011. "Against Space: Place, Movement, Knowledge." In *Boundless Worlds: An Anthropological Approach to Movement*, edited by Peter Kirby, 29–44. New York: Berghahn Books.

———. 2010. *Bringing Things to Life: Creative Entanglements in a World of Materials*. Working Paper #15. http://eprints.ncrm.ac.uk/1306/1/0510_creative_entanglements.pdf

———. 2007. *Lines: A Brief History.* New York: Routledge.

———. 2000. *The Perception of the Environment: Essays on Livelihood, Dwelling and Skill.* London: Routledge.

International Labor Organization. 1972. *Employment, Incomes and Equality: A Strategy for Increasing Productive Employment in Kenya.* Geneva: International Labor Office.

International Telecommunication Union. 2019. *Online Statistics.* Accessed August 7, 2019. http://www.itu.int/ITU-D/ICTEYE/Indicators/Indicators.aspx

———. 2008. *Online Statistics.* Retrieved August 7, 2008. http://www.itu.int/ITU-D/ICTEYE/Indicators/Indicators.aspx

———. 2001. *Effective Regulation. Case Study: Morocco* Accessed May 15, 2002. http://www.itu.int/osg/spu/casestudies/#regulation

Ito, Mizuko, Daisuke Okabe, and Ken Anderson. 2011. "Portable Objects in Three Cities: The Personalization of Urban Places." In *The Reconstruction of Time and Space,* edited by Rich Ling and Scott Campbell, 67–87. London: Transaction Publishers.

Ito, Mizuko, Daisuke Okabe, and Misa Matsuda, eds. 2005. *Personal, Portable, Pedestrian: Mobile Phones in Japanese Life.* Cambridge, MA: The MIT Press.

James, Jeffrey. 2006. *Information Technology and Development: A New Paradigm for Delivering the Internet to Rural Areas in Developing Countries.* New York: Routledge

Jensen, Robert. 2007. "The Digital Provide: Information (Technology), Market Performance, and Welfare in the South Indian Fisheries Sector." *The Quarterly Journal of Economics* 122, no. 3: 879–924.

Kapchan, Deborah. 1996. *Gender on the Market: Moroccan Women and the Revoicing of Tradition.* Philadelphia, PA: University of Pennsylvania Press.

Katz, James, and Satomi Sugiyama. 2005. "Mobile Phones as Fashion Statements: The Co-creation of Mobile Communication's Public Meaning." In *Mobile Communications: Re-negotiating the Social Sphere,* edited by Richard Ling and Per Pedersen, 63–81. London: Springer.

Kavoori, Anandam and Noah Arceneaux, eds. 2006. The *Cell Phone Reader: Essays in Social Transformation.* New York: Peter Lang.

King, Kenneth. 2001. "Africa's Informal Economies: Thirty Years On." *SAIS Review* 21, no. 1: 97–108.

Kriem, Maya. 2009. "Mobile Telephony in Morocco: A Changing Sociality." *Media, Culture & Society* 31, no. 4: 617–632.

Labonne, Julien, and Robert Chase. 2009. *The Power of Information: The Impact of Mobile Phones on Farmers' Welfare in the Philippines.* Policy Research Working Paper No. 4996. Washington, DC: World Bank.

Lahlou, Mehdi. n.d. *Child Labor in Morocco: The Socioeconomic Background of the "Little Maids" Phenomenon.* Rabat: Ministry of Planning. Retrieved September 24, 2019. http://www.araburban.org/ChildCity/Papers/English/Lahlou%20Morocco.pdf

Larson, Goran. 2011. *Muslims and the New Media: Historical and Contemporary Debates.* Burlington, VT: Ashgate.

Latour, Bruno. 2005. *Reassembling the Social: An Introduction to Actor-Network-Theory*. Oxford, UK: Oxford University Press.

———. 1992. "Where Are the Missing Masses? The Sociology of a Few Mundane Artifacts." In *Shaping Technology/Building Society: Studies in Sociotechnical Change*, edited by Wiebe Bijker and John Law, 225–258. Cambridge, MA: The MIT Press.

Lefebvre, Henri. 1991. *The Production of Space*. Oxford: Blackwell.

Lewisohn, Leonard. 2000. "Tawakkul." In *The Encyclopedia of Islam*, edited by P. Bearman, Th. Bianquis, C.E. Bosworth, E. van Donzel, and W.P. Heinrichs, 376–378. Second edition. Volume X. Leiden: E.J. Brill.

Light, Ann. 2011. "Negotiations in Space: The Impact of Receiving Phone Calls on the Move." In *The Reconstruction of Time and Space*, edited by Rich Ling and Scott Campbell, 191–213. London: Transaction Publishers.

Ling, Rich. 2008. *New Tech, New Ties: How Mobile Communication is Reshaping Social Cohesion*. Cambridge, MA: MIT Press.

———. 2004. *The Mobile Connection: The Cell Phone's Impact on Society*. San Francisco, CA: Morgan Kaufmann.

Ling, Rich, and Scott Campbell, eds. 2011. "Introduction: The Reconstruction of Space and Time through Mobile Communication Practices." In *The Reconstruction of Space and Time*, 1–15. London: Transaction Publishers.

Ling, Rich, and Jonathan Donner. 2009. *Mobile Communication*. Malden, MA: Polity Press.

Ling, Rich, and Per Pedersen, eds. 2005. *Mobile Communications: Re-negotiating the Social Sphere*. London: Springer.

Lipset, David. 2018. "A Handset Dangling in a Doorway: Mobile Phone Sharing in a Rural Sepik Village (Papua New Guinea)." In *The Moral Economy of Mobile Phones: Pacific Islands Perspectives*, edited by Robert Foster and Heather Horst, 19–38. Canberra: ANU Press.

Liu, Jun. 2017. "Mobile Phones, Social Ties and Collective Action Mobilization in China." *Acta Sociologica* 60, no. 3: 213–227.

Malaval, Philippe, and Bernard Shadeck. 2000. *Marketing, facteur de développement: L'émergence des pays du Sud*. Paris, France: Editions L'Harmattan.

Malinowski, Bronislaw. 1961[1922]. *Argonauts of the Western Pacific*. New York: Dutton.

Maroon, Bahiyyih. 2006. "Mobile Sociality in Urban Morocco." *In The Cell Phone Reader: Essays in Social Transformation*, edited by Anandam Kavoori and Noah Arceneaux, 189–203. New York: Peter Lang.

Masbah, Mohamed. 2018. *"Let it Spoil": Morocco's Boycott and the Empowerment of the "Regular" Citizen*. Doha, Qatar: Aljazeera Center for Studies. Retrieved October 10, 2020. https://studies.aljazeera.net/en/reports/2018/11/181114115931285.html

Massey, Doreen. 2005. *For Space*. London: Sage.

Mauss, Marcel. 1990 [1925]. *The Gift: The Form and Reason for Exchange in Archaic Societies*. London: Routledge.

McLuhan, Marshall. 1971. *Understanding Media: The Extensions of Man*. New York: McGraw-Hill Company.

McMillan, John. 2002. *Reinventing the Bazaar: The Natural History of Markets*. New York: W. W. Norton & Company.

McMurray, David. 2001. *In and Out of Morocco: Smuggling and Migration in a Frontier Boomtown*. Minneapolis, MN: University of Minnesota Press.

Menin, Laura. 2018. "Texting Romance: Mobile Phones, Intimacy and Gendered Moralities in Central Morocco." *Contemporary Levant* 3, no. 1: 66–78.

Mernissi, Fatima. 1997. *The Forgotten Queens of Islam*. Minneapolis, MN: University of Minnesota Press.

———. 1982a. "Zhor's World: A Moroccan Domestic Servant Speaks Out." *Gender Issues* 2, no. 1: 3–31.

———. 1982b. "Women and the Impact of Capitalist Development in Morocco Part I." *Gender Issues* 2, no. 2: 64–104.

Miller, D., L.A. Rabho, P. Awondo, M. de Vries, M. Duque, P. Garvey, L. Haapio-Kirk, C. Hawkins, A. Otaegui, S. Walton, and X. Wang. 2021. *The Global Smartphone: Beyond a Youth Technology*. London: UCL Press.

Miller, Daniel, and Don Slater. 2000. *The Internet: An Ethnographic Approach*. Oxford, UK: Berg.

Ministère du Plan. 2014. *Population Légale du Maroc: Le Recensement Général de la Population et de l'Habitat*. Rabat, Morocco: Direction de la Statistique.

Moaddel, Mansoor. 2002. "The Study of Islamic Culture and Politics: An Overview and Assessment." *Annual Review of Sociology* 28: 359–386.

Molony, Thomas. 2008. "Running Out of Credit: The Limitations of Mobile Telephony in a Tanzanian Agricultural Marketing System." *Journal of African Studies* 46, no. 4: 637–658.

Montgomery, Mary. 2019. *Hired Daughters: Domestic Workers among Ordinary Moroccans*. Bloomington, IN: Indiana University Press.

Muto, Megumi, and Takashi Yamano. 2009. "The Impact of Mobile Phone Coverage Expansion on Market Participation: Panel Data Evidence from Uganda." *World Development* 37, no. 12: 1887–1896.

Napora, John. 2011. "Sanctity, Social Distance, and the Price of Cloth in a Moroccan Suq." In *Textile Economies: Power and Value from the Local to the Transnational*, edited by Walter E. Little and Patricia A. McAnany, 181–200. Lanham, MD: Rowman & Littlefield Publishers.

Ostrom, Elinor. 1990. *Governing the Commons: The Evolution of Institutions for Collective Action*. Cambridge, UK: Cambridge University Press.

Özkul, Didem. 2017. "Placing Mobile Ethnography: Mobile Communication as a Practice of Placemaking." In *The Routledge Companion of Digital Ethnography*, edited by Larissa Hjort, Heather Horst, Anne Galloway, and Genevieve Bell, 221–232. New York: Routledge.

Pelto, Pertti. 1973. *The Snowmobile Revolution: Technology and Social Change in the Arctic*. Menlo Park, CA: Cummings.

Pelto, Pertti, and Ludger Müller-Wille. 1972. "Snowmobiles: Technological Revolution in the Arctic." In *Technology and Social Change*, edited H. Russell Bernard and Pertti J. Pelto, 166–199. New York: The Macmillan Company.

Pfaffenberger, Bryan. 1992. "Social Anthropology of Technology." *Annual Review of Anthropology* 21: 491–516.

Pinch, Trevor, and Wiebie Bijker. 1987. "The Social Construction of Facts and Artifacts: Or How the Sociology of Science and the Sociology of Technology Might Benefit Each Other." In *The Social Construction of Technological Systems*, edited by Wiebie Bijker, Thomas Hughes, and Trevor Pinch, 17–50. Cambridge, MA: The MIT Press.

Polanyi, Karl, Conrad Arensberg, and harry Pearson, eds. 1957. *Trade and Market in the Early Empires: Economies in History and Theory*. Glencoe, IL: The Free Press.

Prahalad, Coimbatore, and Allen Hammond. 2002. "Serving the Poor, Profitably." *Harvard Business Review* 80, no. 9: 48–57.

Prahalad, Coimbatore, and Stuart Hart. 2002. "The Fortune at the Bottom of the Pyramid." *Strategy+Business* 26: 54–67.

Putnam, Robert. 2000. *Bowling Alone: The Collapse and Revival of American Community*. New York: Simon & Schuster.

Rachik, Abderrahmane. 2016. *La Société contre l'état: Mouvements sociaux et stratégie de la rue au Maroc*. Casablanca, Morocco: Éditions La Croisée des Chemins.

Rangaswamy, Nimmi, and Payal Arora. 2016. "The Mobile Internet in the Wild and Every Day: Digital Leisure in the Slums of Urban." *International Journal of Cultural Studies* 19, no. 6: 611–626.

Rheingold, Howard. 2002. *Smart Mobs: The Next Social Revolution*. Cambridge, MA: Basic Books.

Rodrik, Dani. 2006. "Goodbye Washington Consensus, Hello Washington Confusion? A Review of the World Bank's Economic Growth Reforms in the 1990s: Learning from a Decade of Reforms." *Journal of Economic Literature* XLIV: 973–987.

Röller, Lars-Hendrik, and Leonard Waverman. 2001. "Telecommunications Infrastructure and Economic Development: A Simultaneous Approach." *American Economic Review* 91, no. 4: 909–923.

Rosen, Lawrence. 1984. *Bargaining for Reality: The Construction of Social Relations in a Muslim Community*. Chicago: University of Chicago Press.

Samuel, Jonathan, Niraj Shah, and Wenona Hadingham. 2005. *Mobile Communications in South Africa, Tanzania, and Egypt: Results from Community and Business Surveys*. Retrieved July 9, 2008. http://www.vodafone.com/etc/medialib/attachments/cr_downloads.Par.78351.File.dat/GPP_SIM_paper_3.pdf.

Schiffer, Michael, eds. 2001. *Anthropological Perspectives on Technology*. Albuquerque, NM: University of New Mexico Press.

Sclove, Richard. 1995. *Democracy and Technology*. New York: Guilford Press.

Sen, Amartya. 2000. *Development as Freedom*. New York: Anchor Books.

Servaes, Jan, ed. 2014. *Technological Determinism and Social Change: Communication in a Tech-mad World*. Lanham, MD: Lexington Books.

Sharabi, Hisham. 1963. "Power and Leadership in the Arab World." *ORBIS: A Journal of World Affairs* 7, no. 3: 583–595.

Sherry, John, and Tony Salvador. 2001. "Running and Grimacing: The Struggle for Balance in Mobile Work." In *Wireless World: Social and Interactional Aspects of the Mobile Age*, edited by Barry Brown, Nicola Green, and Richard Harper, 108–120. London: Springer.

Sherry, John, Tony Salvador, and Hsain Ilahiane. 2003. "Navigating Multiple Networks: ICTs, Multinationals and Development." In *Connected for Development: Information Kiosks and Sustainability*, edited by Akhtar Badshah, Sarbuland Khan, and Maria Garrido, 25–34. New York: United Nations Information and Communication Technologies Task Force, ICT Task Force Series 4.

Sommerfelt, Tone, ed. 2001. *Domestic Child Labour in Morocco: An Analysis of the Parties Involved in Relationships to "Petites Bonnes"*. Oslo, Norway: Fafo Institute for Applied Social Science. Retrieved September 23, 2019. http://www.fafo.no/pub/370.pdf

Sreberny-Mohammadi, Annabelle, and Ali Mohammadi. 1994. *Small Media, Big Revolution: Communication, Culture, and the Iranian Revolution*. Minneapolis, MN: University of Minnesota Press.

Stoller, Paul. 1996. "Spaces, Places, and Fields: The Politics of West African Trading in New York City's Informal Economy." *American Anthropologist* 98, no. 4: 776–788.

Sullivan, Nicholas. 2007. You *Can Hear Me Now: How Microloans and Cell Phones are Connecting the World's Poor to the Global Economy*. New York: John Wiley & Sons, Inc.

Tenhunen, Sirpa. 2008. "Mobile Technology in the Village: ICTs, Culture, and Social Logistics in India." *Journal of the Royal Anthropological Institute* 14, no. 3: 515–534.

Townsend, Anthony. 2000. "Life in the Real: Mobile Telephones and Urban Metabolism." *Journal of Urban Technology* 7, no. 2: 85–104.

United Nations Development Program. 2020. *Global Knowledge Index*. Accessed July 7, 2021. https://www.undp.org/publications/global-knowledge-index-2020

———. 2019. *Human Development Report. Beyond Income, Beyond Averages, Beyond Today: Inequalities in Human Development in the 21st Century*. Accessed August 7, 2019. http://hdr.undp.org/sites/default/files/hdr2019.pdf.

———. 2018. *Making Data Work for Human Development*. Accessed June 17, 2019. http://hdr.undp.org/en/content/making-data-work-human-development.

———. 2003a. *Arab Human Development Report: Building a Knowledge Society*. Accessed March 20, 2004.

———. 2003b. *Development Report: Millennium Development Goals: A Compact among Nations to End Human Poverty Human*. Accessed March 20, 2004. http://hdr.undp.org/en/reports/global/hdr2003/ .

———. 2001. *Human Development Report. Making New Technologies Work for Human Development*. Retrieved May 19, 2002. http://hdr.undp.org/reports/global/2001/en/

Verbeek, Peter Paul. 2005. "Artifacts and Attachment: A Post-script Philosophy of Mediation." In *Inside the Politics of Technology*, edited by H. Harbers, 125–146. Amsterdam: Amsterdam University Press.

Wardlow, Holly. 2018. "HIV, Phone Friends and Affective Technology in Paua New Guinea." In *The Moral Economy of Mobile Phones: Pacific Islands Perspectives*, edited by Robert Foster and Heather Horst, 39–52. Canberra: ANU Press.

Waterbury, John. 1972. *North for the Trade: The Life & Times of a Berber Merchant.* Berkeley, CA: University of California Press.

Weber, Maximillian. 1968a. *Economy and society.* New York: Bedminster Press Incorporated.

———. 1968b. *On Charisma and Institution Building. In Selected Papers,* S. N. Eisenstadt, ed. Chicago: University of Chicago Press.

———. 1958. The *Protestant Ethic and the Spirit of Capitalism.* New York: Scribner's Press.

Wehr, Hans. 1979. *A Dictionary of Modern Written Arabic.* Wiesbaden: Otto Harrassowitz.

Wellman, Barry. 2002. *Little Boxes, Glocalization, and Networked Individualism.* http://calchong.tripod.com/sitebuildercontent/sitebuilderfiles/LittleBoxes.pdf.

———. 2001. "Physical Place and CyberPlace: The Rise of Personalized Networking." *International Journal of Urban and Regional Research* 25, no. 2: 227–252.

Westermarck, Edward. 1968 [1926]. *Ritual and Belief in Morocco.* Vols. 1 and 2. New Hyde Park, NY: University Books.

Whitaker, Mark. 2016. "Amiable and Agonistic Incoherence in Sri Lanka and the Tamil Diaspora." Paper presented at the American Ethnological Society Meetings. Washington, DC, April 1.

Wilken, Rowan. 2011. *Teletechnologies, Place, and Community.* New York: Routledge.

Wilken, Rowan, and Girard Goggin, eds. 2012. *Mobile Technologies and Place.* New York: Routledge.

Williamson, John. 2000. "What the World Bank Should Think about the Washington Consensus?" *World Bank Research Observer* 15, no. 2: 251–264.

Winner, Langdon. 1980. "Do Artifacts Have Politics?" *Daedalus* 109, no.1: 121–136.

World Bank. 2016. *World Development Report: Digital Dividends.* Retrieved May 3, 2018. https://www.worldbank.org/en/publication/wdr2016

———. 2013. *ICT in Agriculture: Source Book.* Retrieved August 20, 2020. http://www.ictinagriculture.org/sourcebook/module-3-mobile-devices-and-their-impact

Index

About the Author

Hsain Ilahiane is professor of anthropology and head of the Department of Anthropology and Middle Eastern Cultures at Mississippi State University. He is the author of *Ethnicities, Community Making, and Agrarian Change: The Political Ecology of a Moroccan Oasis* (2004) and *Historical Dictionary of the Berbers (Imazighen)* (2017).

Milton Keynes UK
Ingram Content Group UK Ltd.
UKHW021350220823
427290UK00023B/301

9 781793 616609